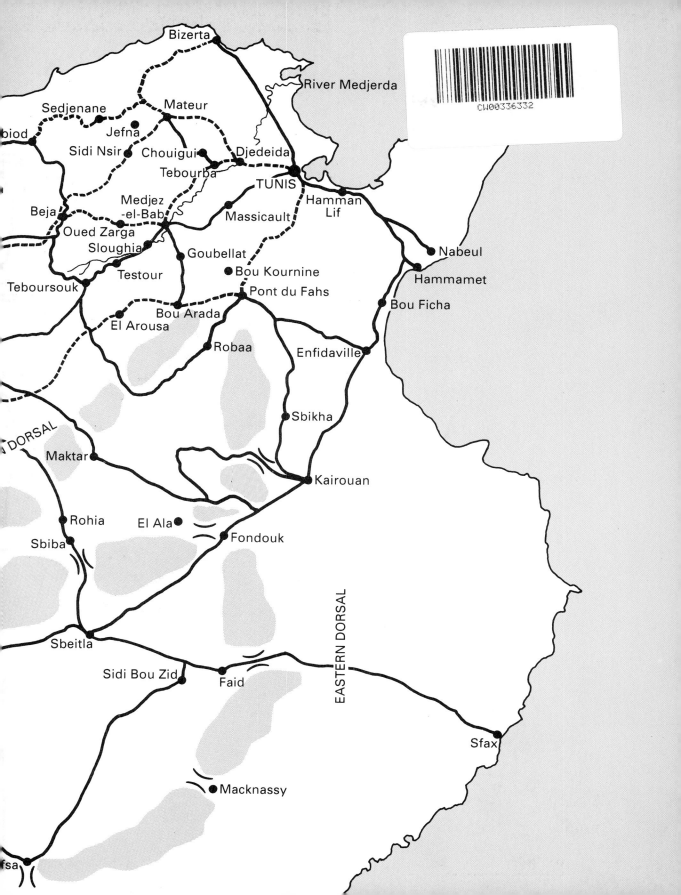

Bizerta

River Medjerda

Sedjenane · Mateur

biod · Jefna

Sidi Nsir · Chouigui · Djedeida

Tebourba

TUNIS

Medjez -el-Bab · Massicault · Hamman Lif

Beja

Oued Zarga

Sloughia · Goubellat · Nabeul

Testour · Bou Kournine · Hammamet

Teboursouk · Pont du Fahs · Bou Ficha

Bou Arada

El Arousa

Robaa · Enfidaville

Sbikha

DORSAL

Maktar · Kairouan

Rohia · El Ala

Sbiba · Fondouk

EASTERN DORSAL

Sbeitla

Sidi Bou Zid · Faid

Sfax

Macknassy

fsa

ACTION FRONT!

A History of 'C' Battery HAC
in War and Peace

James Colquhoun

Bill Tullberg

With best wishes

James Colquhoun — 2/7/92

Leo Cooper

This book is dedicated to the memory of all those who served in 'C' Battery in war and peace and died before their time.

© James Colquhoun, 1992
First published in Great Britain 1992 by Leo Cooper, 190 Shaftesbury Avenue,
London WC2H 8JL, an imprint of Pen & Sword Books Ltd, 47 Church Street,
Barnsley, S. Yorks. S70 2AS.

ISBN 0 85052 270 6

Design and production in association with Book Production Consultants, Cambridge

Typeset by KeyStar, St Ives, Cambridge

Paper most generously supplied by Pegg Haindl Ltd.
Services and assistance by Express Newspapers plc

Printed by St Edmundsbury Press, Bury St Edmunds, Suffolk.

Contents

	Foreword	iv
	Author's acknowledgements	v
CHAPTER ONE	*If you want peace, prepare for war*	1
CHAPTER TWO	*Training for war*	7
CHAPTER THREE	*Stiffening the sinews*	17
CHAPTER FOUR	*Blade Force*	28
CHAPTER FIVE	*Tunisian victory*	45
CHAPTER SIX	*Distant drums*	63
CHAPTER SEVEN	*Sempre avanti*	73
CHAPTER EIGHT	*Grande finale in Emilia*	88
CHAPTER NINE	*Valiant hearts*	94
CHAPTER TEN	*'C' Battery at home*	99
CHAPTER ELEVEN	*Last post*	113
APPENDIX A	*The Roll of Honour*	123
APPENDIX B	*Honours and Awards*	125
APPENDIX C	*'C' Battery 1939–1945*	127
APPENDIX D	*'C' Battery 12th (HAC) Regiment RHA*	130
APPENDIX E	*'C' Battery 1947–1973*	133
APPENDIX F	*'C' Battery Commanders and Camps 1947–1973*	138
	Sources and references	139
	Bibliography	141
	Abbreviations	142
	List of sponsors	143
	Index	144

Foreword

Here is the story of 'C' Battery HAC. In the annals of the Honourable Artillery Company through the centuries, perhaps the 34 years during which 'C' Battery HAC served their sovereign and the nation may seem relatively short. But what years they were!

From its very beginnings, its embodiment, and the finding of its unique identity and strong sense of purpose, through its early training and equipping for the rigours of battle until it was honed into 'a very formidable weapon of war', to the serious business of campaigning and then, later, to the more light-hearted days of peacetime soldiering, the whole being of 'C' was steeped in the very essence of the volunteer spirit – a spirit which infused all those who served in the Battery, whether they were pre-war members of the Territorial Army, regulars who were posted in from time to time, those who were 'in for the duration' or those who joined its ranks during the years of the Cold War.

The record of gallantry of the Battery in the Second World War, so vividly recounted in this volume, during the sustained and fierce fighting in North Africa and, later, in the hard slog up the spine of Italy, is one to stir the imagination of the romantic and appeal to the interest of the professional soldier, not least the Gunner. Then, after the upheaval of disbandment for some and reorganization for others, when the war ended, the Battery continued in its service for another 26 years, during which it faithfully trained and prepared itself for any eventuality that might well have come its way: and it enjoyed itself – hugely!

For members of this great Battery with us still today, the story of its exploits, and especially of those who gave their lives for their country, is a testimonial: a memorial of duty very well done. For those of us who were otherwise preoccupied and who did not have the honour of serving in 'C' but who can, by association, take pride in its record, we have an evocation and an inspiration. For those who have yet to serve in the Honourable Artillery Company in future years, the actions of 'C' Battery HAC will be a constant reminder of what service in the Company is all about, of what it demands of each of us – a truly fine example.

General Sir Richard Trant KCB
Colonel Commandant
Honourable Artillery Company

Author's acknowledgements

I have never had much sympathy with the old soldier's advice that one should never volunteer for anything and so when Major Basil Bicknell TD asked me nearly two years ago if I would write this book, I willingly agreed. I realized immediately that I would be firing on unmapped ranges, but that was the challenge. I could have achieved very little, though, were it not for the immense amount of support and help which I received from so many people.

I would first of all like to thank Basil Bicknell, who has been the driving force behind this book and has at all times given me unstinting and cheerful support. In this he has been much helped by Colonel Graeme Gilchrist TD, Geoffrey Hyatt and Simon Morgan. My task was made considerably easier by Ian Miller, who kindly lent me Lt Colonel Stanley Rae's unpublished history of 12th HAC Regiment RHA together with his (Ian Miller's) photographic albums, which contain pictures and names of everyone in 'C' Battery in 1942 and 1943.

I was greatly assisted in my desire to put over the Gunner's point of view during the war by Gordon Thomas and Allan Lewis, who both offered me their wartime memories written in their own inimitable styles. I was presented with real treasure troves by Colonel Aubrey Lincoln MC TD and Colonel Mike Austin-Smith CBE MC TD. These two officers, together with Brigadier Ken Hunt OBE MC, Brigadier Shelford Bidwell OBE FRHists and Colonel Geoffrey Armstrong DSO MC TD, not only gave me valuable advice but also very carefully read my manuscript. I am extremely grateful to all of them.

I would like to thank my old friend Leo Cooper for allowing us to use his prestigious imprint and he, together with Adrian Rowbotham who designed the dust jacket, has given so much help and has tried to keep me on the straight and narrow historical path.

I must also thank the cheerful and competent team at Book Production Consultants, especially Tony Littlechild, Roz Williams, Jim Reader and Tricia Rowland.

The maps were drawn by Steve Freeman and Dave Edridge and are designed to give the reader a clear idea of the geography which affected 'C' Battery in particular rather than of the campaigns they fought in as a whole. The typesetting for the maps was generously provided by Flowery Typesetters Ltd.

I thank John Attwood for all the time he spent checking the index cards of members of 12th HAC Regiment RHA and building up the list of names of members of the Battery. He was able to obtain access to these records through the kind permission of Ken Bishop of the Old Comrades Association.

The photographs which appear on pages 22, 51, 58, 59, 64, 77, 78, 83 and 91 are reproduced by courtesy of the Imperial War Museum. The picture of Generalmajor Fischer on page 38 is reproduced by courtesy of the Bundesarchiv, Koblenz. The picture of Major Michael Gilbert on page 86 is by Mark

Gerson. The picture of Bodney Camp on page 105 is reproduced by courtesy of Khyber Studios, North Bodney.

The poem 'The Naming of Parts' is reprinted from Henry Reed's *Collected Poems*, edited by Jon Stallworthy (1991), by permission of Oxford University Press. The poem by Captain M.J. Pugh RA is reproduced by courtesy of the Royal Artillery Institution. 'A Day in the Life' by Lennon and McCartney (copyright Northern Songs) is reproduced by courtesy of MCA Music Ltd; all rights controlled and administered by MCA Music Ltd under licence from Northern Songs. The poems 'A Musing upon Being Embodied' by Douglas Street and 'Troopship' by Ted Lane are reproduced from *More Poems of the Second World War: The Oasis Collection*, published by J.M. Dent on behalf of the Salamander Oasis Trust.

I am also grateful to everyone who has patiently answered my questions, read my manuscript, given me interviews, written letters to me and generally helped me in one way or another. These include: Colonel Drummond Angus TD, Captain Howard Atherton MC, Major Peter Barshall TD, Mrs D. Barstow, Captain Michael Baylis, Bob Breen, John Burns, Alan Colquhoun, Sebastian Colquhoun, Peter Corke, Major Peter Davidson-Smith TD, Guy Edmunds, Robert Elphick, Jack Farmer, Mike Gee, Major Michael Gilbert CBE TD LLB, David Girling, Mrs H.I. Grose, Tom Hartman, Major Ian Hartigan, Major Bill Hebblethwaite, Roddy Hill-Smith, Captain David Horn (Curator of the Guards Museum), Tim Jacques, Captain Geoffrey Lloyd CBE RN, Michael Miller, John Montgomery (Royal United Services Institute), Wilfred Picton-Turbervill, Colonel Paul Pettit CBE MC TD, Major Don Pryce MBE, Julian Seddon, Major Jack Sewell MC, Brigadier and Mrs K.A. Timbers (Royal Artillery Institution), Mrs Jean Tsushima (HAC Archivist), Major Derrick Walker TD and Eddie Webb.

Lastly I have to thank two ladies. The first is Lucy Cannon, who has typed my manuscript with unfailing patience and good humour. The second is my wife Rosanagh, who has not only tolerantly put up with my unsociable behaviour whilst writing this book, but also used her experience of proofreading and knowledge of English grammar to correct my many mistakes.

Whilst every effort has been made to check the facts and names mentioned in this book, I hope the reader will understand that inevitably there will be errors based on lack of information and the fallibility of memory.

JAMES COLQUHOUN
March 1992

CHAPTER ONE

If you want peace, prepare for war

Before the end of August
I officered in TA,
A sort of half-civilian
In an especial way,
But now that I'm embodied,
I'm a different sort of bloke,
I'm now a sort of regular –
Believe me that's no joke!

I've newly been embodied,
Is my brand new body's form
A comely one and manly –
Or just my shoddy norm?
When I am disembodied –
I hope one Victory Day –
Will I become civilian
And be an ex-TA?

Or when disembodied
In God's especial way,
Been killed, and sent to 'transit camp',
Till I am re-embodied
On Judgement Day?

Douglas Street
A musing upon being embodied
TA Drill Hall, 1939

B y the spring of 1939 Europe was in a ferment. Hitler's Nazi Germany was on the war path. In the previous 12 months Hitler had annexed Austria (March 1938) and his troops had taken over the German-populated areas of Czechoslovakia known as the Sudetenland on 1 October 1938. The week before that, at a meeting in Munich Hitler had lulled the British Prime Minister Neville Chamberlain into thinking that he had negotiated 'peace in our time'. But it was only in March 1939, when German troops finally occupied the remainder of Czechoslovakia, that Chamberlain realized how badly he had been duped.

> On March 29th Mr Chamberlain announced in Parliament the planned doubling to the Territorial Army, including an increase on paper of 210,000 men (unequipped). On April 3, Keitel, Hitler's Chief of Staff, issued the secret 'Directive for the Armed Forces 1939–40', in regard to Poland – 'Case White' was the code name. The Führer added the following directions 'Preparations must be made in such a way that the operations can be carried out at any time from September 1st onwards'.[1]

The effect of those events on the most senior regiment in the Territorial Army, the Honourable Artillery Company, was profound. In fact, by the time the duplication of the Territorial Army had been announced, the HAC was already recruiting for what became the 86th Heavy Anti-Aircraft Regiment (HAC) Royal Artillery.

At that time the HAC was composed of the Infantry Battalion and 'A' and 'B' Batteries of Royal Horse Artillery. The Infantry Battalion was subsequently converted into the 162nd (HAC) Officer Cadet Training Unit, and 'A' and 'B' Batteries became 11th (HAC) Regiment RHA. 'A' and 'B' Batteries were also required to provide a cadre of officers and NCOs to start up another new regiment, the title of which caused some controversy.

The initial decision to refer to them as Second Line Batteries or Duplicate A or Duplicate B batteries was ignominious. Nor was the title for the new regiment of HAC No. 2 Regiment RHA (TA) seen to be anything but clumsy. For the new Regiment was determined that it was not going to be second to anyone, just as 'C' Battery would never own up to being a duplicate of 'A' Battery then or ever! Thus in a short time the title of the 12th Regiment RHA (HAC) TA was confirmed with 'C' and 'D' Batteries and RHQ.

The aim was to bring both regiments up to the war strength of 463 all ranks as opposed to the peace establishment of only 279.

It was, and still is the custom of the Company that all candidates for admission to the membership must be sponsored and seconded by existing members. The sponsor recommends his candidate to the Court of Assistants (the equivalent of a Committee) and on the candidate being approved, he is required to pro-

Embodiment Notice of Wilfred Picton-Turbervill.

Substitution for A.F. E 635

Notice to Join

E M B O D I M E N T

Rank and Name .....Gnr. Picton. Turbervill W.......

Battery   Honourable Artillery Company

Whereas the Army Council, in pursuance of His Majesty's Proclamation have directed that the Honourable Artillery Company (Artillery) be embodied on the 1st. Sept. 1939. You are hereby required to attend at Armoury House, Finsbury London E.C.1. not later than 10.00 hours o'clock 2nd Sept. 1939 Should you not present yourself as ordered you will be liable to be proceeded against. You should comply with the instructions contained in your Army Book 3 (Territorial Army Soldiers ' Pocket Book) Regarding procedure on being called out for service , and disposal of your National Insurance Card and Unemployment Book. If married you should complet the statement of Family Particulars in the Pocket Book before you leave home, and bring that book with you ready to be handed in when you report for duty,

.............................for Adjutant.

Honourable Artillery Company

Date 1st. Sept.1939

claim a solemn declaration of loyalty to the Captain General (the reigning monarch) and the Honourable Artillery Company.

This process put great stress on the Court of Assistants who found themselves in almost nightly session and between 27 March and 15 May 1939, 1300 new members were admitted. Tents and huts sprouted at the southern end of the playing fields outside Armoury House and not a day went past without the old or new units mustering for training.

It was therefore no doubt with a feeling of some weariness that Captain Drummond D. Angus commanded his first parade of 'C' Battery on 15 May 1939. He recalled his impressions at that time in a letter to the author:

Recruits flocked in and were signed on. I was presented with a list of names with the briefest of details. I remember spending a weekend at Armoury House with a recently posted PSI going through those names, card-indexing them and picking NCOs by the simple process of promoting anyone who had had the remotest experience of e.g. School OTC or similar.

We paraded weekly in mufti and weaponless of course, but I forget how I kept them interested.

Fortunately, the *'C' Battery Notes* were published four times in the HAC *Journal* before censorship precluded their continuation; they give a good idea of the well-intentioned but rather impractical endeavour of those days. The first *'C' Battery Notes* are worth reproducing in full and show, right from the start, the same somewhat whimsical style which was adopted by post-war scribes. The reader will also note the declaration of intent in the last sentence. The flame of 'C' Battery's spirit had been ignited.

Counting ourselves lucky to have scraped past the Recruiting Committee, who regarded us more in sorrow than in anger, we were duly impressed by the solemn ceremony before the Court of Assistants and queued up to sign the Vellum Book. Our first impression of soldiering, after having been admitted to the Company, was of the enormous amount of clerical work involved, for we then proceeded to fill up innumerable forms in relays and by numbers.

By the time we held our first parade, the 'Duplicate A' Battery was complete, and on May 15th we assembled and were divided into eight subsections. This seemed as pleasant a way of spending the evening as any. Captain Angus, who introduced himself to us as our Commanding Officer, surveyed our somewhat motley ranks with an expression of which despair was nearly, but not quite, the chief ingredient. One gunner at least thought he detected an anticipatory gleam of things to come in the eye which regarded the ranks.

Since then, we have had four parades (up to the end of May), two of which were devoted to providing an audience on which would-be lecturers could practise the art of oratory. One or two useful tips on the science of heckling were picked up, and a good time was had by all – except the lecturers.

On the last day of the month we paraded with 'B/2' and heard a fascinating talk from Major Goold Walker on the history of the Company. It provided an admirable background to our activities and certainly inspired many recruits with a determination to reach the level of efficiency, endurance and courage of which we had heard such stirring examples.

Progress to date can be summed up in three items of knowledge acquired during our five evenings at Armoury House:

1. That a certain book of statistics (the subject of which has escaped the writer's mind) is indispensable.
2. Not to use the hands when demonstrating the appearance of open sights.
3. To ask for a three-and-a-half when one wants a bitter.

Although it is very early days yet to report tremendous progress, it may be said that, if keenness and the will to learn count for anything, the elder brothers of 'C' will soon have to look to their laurels.[2]

Major Drummond Angus was the first Battery Commander of 'C' Battery. He commanded the Battery from May to September 1939.

By the end of June, by parading twice a week on Wednesdays and Fridays, 'C' Battery had come to feel it had an identity of its own. The main problem about training was the lack of equipment in any form. The Battery had no uniforms, and had to borrow 'A' Battery's 18-pounders when they could. The Battery scribe noted:

> As for gun drill, we get in as much as possible when nobody is using the guns and the issue of gents' natty garage suiting by a beneficent authority prevents our ill-used civilian attire from suffering further wear and tear – and swear.

At this time, 12th Regiment hoped to go to Salisbury Plain for a fortnight's camp on 9 September.

> With this aim in view, we are now being instructed in our various duties, and the excellent spirit of the Battery was demonstrated when volunteers were wanted for drivers. Not a man held back!
>
> By September 23rd, when we leave camp, troops are 'to be able to operate independently in the field'. We extend our sympathy to the officers![3]

But history was to forestall these expectations. On 25 August, 129 other ranks of 12th Regiment were embodied as a 'key party' and by the end of the month the Regiment had reached full strength. On the evening of 1 September 1939 all ranks were called up by announcements made by the BBC. Saturday 2 September was spent collecting personnel and issuing cash grants for kit. All ranks were dismissed at the end of the day and ordered to parade the following day. That night it rained but the next day saw a lovely sunny Sunday morning and 12th Regiment paraded for a kit inspection. At 11am the Prime Minister, Neville Chamberlain, told the nation on the wireless that Great Britain was at war with Germany. Twenty minutes later this dramatic statement was emphasized by the sound of the first air-raid warning.

All personnel proceeded calmly to the system of trenches which had been dug on the soccer pitch in front of Armoury House. However, the warning was a false alarm and the parade continued. When they were finally dismissed everyone realized that their lives had been irretrievably changed and they must have pondered about what the future had in store.

CHAPTER TWO

Training for war

Today we have naming of parts. Yesterday,
We had daily cleaning. And tomorrow morning,
We shall have what to do after firing? But today,
Today we have naming of parts. Japonica
Glistens like coral in all of the neighbouring gardens,
And today we have naming of parts.

This is the lower sling swivel. And this
Is the upper sling swivel, whose use you will see,
When you are given your slings. And this is the piling swivel,
Which in your case you have not got. The branches
Hold in the gardens their silent, eloquent gestures,
Which in our case we have not got.

This is the safety-catch, which is always released
With an easy flick of the thumb. And please do not let me
See anyone using his finger. You can do it quite easy
If you have any strength in your thumb. The blossoms
Are fragile and motionless, never letting anyone see
Any of them using their finger.

And this you can see is the bolt. The purpose of this
Is to open the breech, as you see. We can slide it
Rapidly backwards and forwards: we call this
Easing the spring. And rapidly backwards and forwards
The early bees are assaulting and fumbling the flowers:
They call it easing the Spring.

They call it easing the Spring: it is perfectly easy
If you have any strength in your thumb: like the bolt,
And the breech, and the cocking-piece, and the point of balance,
Which in our case we have not got; and the almond-blossom
Silent in all of the gardens and the bees going backwards and forwards
For today we have naming of parts.

Naming of parts
Henry Reed

The next 18 months of 'C' Battery's existence was very much a time of uneasy adolescence. The initial concept of duplicating the Territorial Army was fine on paper but totally illusory in fact.

In 1933 there were 580 batteries of TA artillery, excluding coastal defence units. The desire for disarmament and appeasement, which so characterized the 1930s, meant that up to 1938 the Territorial Army was never up to strength. In 1936 a German newspaper the *Münchener Zeitung* commented on the lack of British preparation for defence:

> Again, the small Regular Army shows a large deficiency about one whole division and the Territorial Army (a sort of Sunday School for amateur soldiers) is so far below its authorized numbers it cannot in any way be considered an effective combatant force.[1]

The decision, taken after Munich, to double the Territorial Army meant trying to raise another 13 divisions to make 26 divisions altogether, to reinforce a regular army of only 6 divisions. This put enormous strain on the slender resources of the regular army. In his book *Gunners at War*, Brigadier Shelford Bidwell describes the difficulties the army faced.

He explains that the problems of training the Territorial Army fell into two areas. One was discipline and the other equipment. Although the description of the TA as a sort of Sunday School would have been seen by many to be gratuitously insulting, there was an element of truth about it. For the TA was that typically British institution, a volunteer organization, comprising public-spirited men who gave up their free time to train as soldiers. Their discipline was a relaxed one and they liked to be praised if they did things right but resented criticism if things went wrong. In addition, their attitude of robust amateurism was simply not sufficient to compete with a really ruthless and professional enemy. As for equipment, there was none. The cupboard was bare, and after the disaster of May 1940, the situation was appalling.

But although the outlook was extremely gloomy, there were glimmers of hope. First, there was the fact that the TA did provide an established framework for expansion, based on traditions of regimental pride. Second, the quality of the volunteers who had responded to the call to arms was of a very high order.

The HAC had the good fortune to attract a large number of these fine volunteers, who readily identified themselves with the Company's motto *Arma Pacis Fulcra*, meaning Peace through Armed Strength, and had as its *raison d'être* the setting-up of soldiers in the defence of the monarchy and the country's constitution. This was a policy which it had been following for over 400 years and its members, new and old, never lacked spirit. It was not their fault that there was little in the way of weapons, transport, equipment or even ammunition with which to protect their homeland, and it will be seen that it took two whole years to provide 12th Regiment with up-to-date weapons and equipment.

Nevertheless, now that the 'balloon had gone up', it took very little time for 12th Regiment to prepare itself and, after several days of hurried goodbyes to friends and relatives, it moved into billets at Borehamwood, near Elstree in Hertfordshire, and took over the then deserted film studios.

The Regiment was commanded by Lt Colonel G.R.N. Heseltine MC. In October 1939 Major D.D. Angus was posted as an instructor at 125 OCTU RA in Yorkshire, and handed over command of 'C' Battery to Major O.C. Campbell-Jones. Major Angus had, in 'C' Battery's first five months, imparted through his own energy, humour and character, the first strains of spirit and panache to which the Battery aspired ever afterwards. He did not stay very long at 125 OCTU and was ultimately posted to Burma, where he finished the war commanding 160 Field Regiment RA. Two weeks earlier, Major G.V. Lazenby had been posted to 121 (HAC) OCTU and handed over command of 'D' Battery to Major E.A. Mortleman MC, but this arrangement did not last long, for Major Mortleman was elevated to 2 i/c and his place was taken by one of the most enthusiastic of the HAC pre-war officers, Captain J.A.T. Barstow. But these were not the only changes and, indeed, during the next 12 months there was a considerable turnover of personnel of all ranks.

In the meantime, 'C' Battery tried to make itself comfortable in its new billets, which varied from 'the luxury of tea in bed and What-time-would-you-like-your-shaving-water-Sir? to the comparative hardship of a mattress which, on investigation, proved to be stuffed with potatoes'.[2]

For the next few weeks they trained as best they could with so little equipment. They started to get fit, drilled and went on route marches. On 21 October 1940 a party of 7 officers and 214 NCOs and men left Borehamwood in order to guard vulnerable points in London. These VPs, as they were known, consisted of bridges, tunnels, railway stations, power stations, food depots etc. 'C' Battery, which provided a contingent for those duties, discovered with some amazement that the purpose of these guards was to defend the VPs not against German invasion but rather the IRA.

Twenty-one-year-old Gunner Mike Austin-Smith, whose enthusiasm for life could never be dampened, wrote diligently to his mother and explained, in a letter dated 23 October 1939, his new circumstances while guarding Battersea Bridge:

> I am sitting outside the guard room on the North side of the bridge, which is situated in the yard of an asphalt works, and surrounded by the Fulham Gaslight & Coke works and the Chelsea power Station so the surroundings and atmosphere are not exactly first class. The South Guard Room is in an old derelict Greyhound track. We do one guard at the South and the next at the North.
>
> Until yesterday we mounted 6 sentries at each end, which meant about 21 in the guard room, which was practically impossible, so now we only mount 2 in the

day and these are doubled at night, so some people have gone back to Boreham Wood, but we are here for about 3 weeks.

The guard that was here before us talked a lot about IRAs throwing bricks on to the bridge by means of a catapult and when he had got the range he was going to heave over a bomb, but nothing has happened since we arrived, except one night some barbed wire entanglements were cut.

We all look very business like with tin helmets, greatcoats, fixed bayonets and loaded rifles. Its a bit hard work here, and in the mornings at the billets our kit has to be just so so, and when you are on guard, there is the breakfast to be cooked over a brazier and washing and shaving in the open.

P.S. Our language now that we are on real Active Service has descended into abysmal depths.

The winter of 1939 was a particularly severe one, with temperatures well below freezing, bringing snow, ice and cruel winds. At the end of the war one officer of 12th Regiment recalled those bitter days:

Those members of the Regiment who wear the Defence Medal will feel particularly entitled to it as a decoration well earned when they recall the winter of 1939–40 and all the peculiar discomforts (not to mention dangers) connected with the initial VP.

My own most vivid recollections are connected with snow, rum, and Queens Road (Battersea) Overground Station which it fell to our lot to guard from dangers more imaginary than real during the Christmas season of 1939.

'We all look very businesslike with tin helmets, greatcoats, fixed bayonets and loaded rifles.' 'C' Battery guard at Battersea, October 1939.

An 18-pounder towed by a fire engine, there being no army transport available at Borehamwood in early 1940.

Moving off on a round of visits to sentries at two in the morning, covered from head to foot in every available garment and undergarment for warmth and still feeling cold in the peculiar dank chill which seemed to haunt the arches and viaducts of the Southern railway system: clasping a stone jar of Rum (Service: Drinking) inside one's overcoat and trying not to imagine what would be said if one dropped it or even caused a drop of the precious liquid to be spilt: trudging through the slush in the sidings and tripping over not less than three sets of rails: finally climbing a vertical steel ladder, pushing open a trap door, and pushing up one's head with natural caution since one was about to emerge in between the rails of the main down line.

It was all very well to tell ourselves as we did then, 'This is nothing – just wait till you get on active service'. Now we know better. VPs were far worse.[3]

'C' Battery's guards found themselves guarding a variety of VPs. On 13 January 1940 they guarded the Surrey Docks, but not for long: on 25 January they found themselves guarding an RASC food store at Deptford. At the end of February they moved again, this time to Rotherhithe, which they finally left on 19 March to re-join the Regiment at Borehamwood.

Two weeks after the Battery's return from what had been a boring but nevertheless arduous tour of duty, the Battery Commander Major O.C. Campbell-Jones handed over to Major Paul Pettit. Major Pettit had been the Adjutant up to that time and had added to his reputation by running a rigorous subalterns' and NCOs' course, much to the delight of the gunners, who enjoyed watching the young officers and NCOs being drilled as hard as they were!

The standard of foot, rifle and gun drill was set very high, right at the beginning. There was, in fact, very little else to be done except get fit and try to learn the more complicated techniques of gunnery with very little hardware to practise with. The Regiment possessed one 18-pounder and an assortment of 4.5-inch Howitzers and 18/25-pounders. There was no army transport, so these guns were towed by a whole array of civilian lorries, all of them still proudly bearing the name of their owners, which included breweries, bakers, brick companies and even the fire service!

Gun positions were occupied with wooden tripods when no guns were available. Bombardiers laid their imaginary pieces with dial sights made of wood, aiming at a broomstick with a compass on top for a director. No. 4s loaded imaginary shells and No. 2s slammed imaginary breeches shut. The curious thing is that, although in retrospect these exercises appear to have bordered on pure farce, it did not seem so at the time. There were moments of laughter but, fundamentally, all those involved knew they were training for a serious business; they knew it was going to take time to get the proper equipment, so the sooner they could learn the drills the better.

'C' Battery consisted of men with a wide range of backgrounds and education: clerks, farmers from South America, lawyers, salesmen, mechanics etc., who had joined up in four different ways. Some were original Territorials and

'C' Battery potential officers ('O' Troop) photographed at Skegness just before they were posted to OCTU, 16 May 1940. W.P. Allesbrook, A.I. Anderson, V.W.G. Barrell, J.A.C. Baxter, M.H. Baylis, K.F. Boustred, G.N. Box, M.W. Braithwaite, S.B. De Courcy-Thompson, J.A. Flemming, H.M. Harris, J.E. Hewett, S.B. Ince, D.R. Kelly, J.R. Long, H.N. Meek, J.S. Mundy, G. Paine, H. Pearson, R. Pitt, H. Rice, M. Robinson, P.K. Rooke, A. Rumsey, J.H. Salter, K.M. Sanders, Shenton, L. Slim, W.C.O'D. Waddington, J.M. Wagner, R.D.P. Wilkinson, E.P.K. Willett, M.G. Wilmot, Peter Wood, M.E. Yeoman, J.H. Young.

pursued a lifestyle, which their post-war successors would have easily identified with, driving sports cars, playing rugger and wearing blues to weekend parties. Others were militia men, mostly cockneys, who brought their own inimitable sense of humour with them, referring to their Territorial colleagues as 'top hole clients!' The third group were Reservists – RA and RHA regulars recalled to duty – and the last were volunteers. The 12th HAC Regiment was one of only a few regiments which were allowed to accept volunteer recruits. The minimum age was 23 years, although that did not stop some enthusiasts from joining when they were even younger.

On joining the Regiment, the men were first required to do their basic training in the Depot Troop. This lasted six weeks, under the command of Lt Rowland-Clark and the close attention of BSM D.S. MacLeod (on loan from 'D' Battery). All basic training is tough, but it seemed to the new recruits that the Depot Troop was particularly demanding. One participant claimed he wore out the soles of his army boots during his six-week induction. BSM MacLeod was very much a larger-than-life character. He was an old Harrovian who, among other things, had been a lumberjack in Canada. He joined the HAC before the war and declined to apply for a commission, preferring to be a Warrant Officer; he finally accomplished his ambition to become RSM of 12th Regiment in North Africa. A big man with a gravel voice, he was the terror of the recruits.

The passing-out parades of the Depot Troop were always of a high standard and critically observed, not only by the officers but also by the men already in the batteries. Having passed out, a Gunner could volunteer to join either 'C' or 'D' Battery and BSM MacLeod could not understand why his own 'D' Battery was not so popular! When a Gunner joined 'C' Battery he wore a red flash in his epaulette with the brass letters HAC superimposed on it. 'D' Battery had a blue flash, RHQ a blue-and-red flash, and 'F' Battery, when it was formed, had a green flash. Gunners who had finished their basic training were also allowed to wear blue-and-red forage caps. The basic pay was 14 shillings a week before stoppages.

On 19 April 1940 12th Regiment moved to Skegness in Lincolnshire. The move entailed a long rail journey but everyone was cheerful; when the train stopped at the intermediary stations of Nottingham and Leicester, hundreds of heads popped out of the windows, yelling and singing.

The billets at Skegness were comfortable, and slowly more equipment was produced. Most important, the Regiment was issued with its first proper guns: in May 1940 'W' Troop of 'C' Battery were armed with 4.5-inch Howitzers and 'D' Battery had a troop of 18-pounders. But it was shortly after this that the British Expeditionary Force started its retreat to Dunkirk. Tension was in the air and when the code word for invasion Caesar was announced, 12th Regiment stood to, in order to defend a large part of Lincolnshire. They were hurriedly issued with 10 rounds per rifle on the first day and a further 250 rounds a day later, much to everyone's relief, since no one had had any practice in actually firing a rifle, let alone a 4.5-inch Howitzer! But, after all, it turned out to be a practice warning.

Although training continued at individual, troop and battery level, it was an unsatisfactory time, not only because of a feeling of frustration but also because of the continuous coming and going of personnel. By October 1940 it was estimated that virtually all the original members of the Regiment had moved on to Officer Cadet Units.

Lt Colonel Heseltine was particularly skilful in selecting potential officers and guiding them to an appropriate arm where they could serve best. The potential officers were placed in 'O' Troop for training before they went to OCTU. Thus 259 men passed through 'C' Battery to become officers in various regiments and some even served in the RAF (see Appendix C).

There were six Royal Artillery OCTUs. The first was of particular significance to the HAC since it was formed from the nucleus of the officer-producing classes, which 'A' and 'B' Batteries HAC had set up before the war. The first two intakes of cadets were entirely made up of HAC men and the title of the unit was 121st (HAC) OCTU under the command of Lt Colonel A.H. Burns DSO, with Major G.V. Lazenby, the former Battery Commander of 'D' Battery 12th HAC Regiment, as one of the chief instructors. The unit was originally stationed in Aldershot, but was finally located at Alton Towers in Staffordshire. 122 OCTU was based at Larkhill; 123 OCTU at Catterick; 124 OCTU at Llandrindod Wells; 125 OCTU at Filey near Scarborough to start with, before moving to Ilkley; and 133 OCTU Group, which started at Shrivenham, moved later to Cardigan Bay and was concerned with training cadets for the Anti-Aircraft Command. The training courses lasted five months before cadets were finally commissioned.

The constant posting of men to OCTUs, combined with further moves to new locations at Wragby near Lincoln and Ecton outside Northampton, did not help to settle the Regiment. Despite all these upheavals, morale never faltered, and to boost everyone's spirits a concert was laid on by those who professed a talent. So when the Regiment found itself at Ecton Hall, Northampton, in July 1940, the curtains went up on the following scene, as described by Mike Austin-Smith in a letter of 10 July 1940:

> a chorus line of Gunners wearing battle dress, cigarette holders and identity discs in their eyes instead of monocles, in the style of the Western Brothers, very blazé and slow:

Chorus:	We're the original HAC, All of us sprigs of nobility We're the creme of the smartest and all of us are in Debrett.
Geoff Roland:	I'm Eustace Willoughby but I can stick it, Guard, mess orderly, Inlying Piquet But I ask you is it cricket?
All:	The Original HAC.
Myself:	I'm Parsonly Vere de Vere, Emptying buckets is very small beer, But after all I'm a Bombardier.
All:	The Original HAC.
Ray:	I come from a long line of Peers The Officers, I think are perfect dears They give me leave to look after my shares. The Original HAC.

... and so on for about a dozen verses.

It was at this time that the Regiment benefited from a draft of 2 officers and 60 other ranks who came from 2nd Regiment RHA and had fought well with the BEF in France. Among these men were Sergeants Pearston and Derricott, who joined 'C' Battery and were later promoted to become the Battery Sergeant Major and Troop Sergeant Major of 'X' Troop respectively.

On 7 August 1940 the Regiment moved to Aubries Park, Bulmer, near Sudbury in Suffolk. This move coincided with the Regiment's coming under command of the 1st Armoured Recce Brigade. Training continued, the day starting with Reveille blown by five trumpeters. PT was taken by the zealous, loud-voiced but essentially kind-hearted Sergeant Brazier.

'C' Battery acquired a pet jackdaw, which spent most of its time at the cookhouse. The cooks tried to teach it to talk and say disrespectful things about the Commanding Officer but, being a loyal bird and not wishing to do anything prejudicial to good order and military discipline, the jackdaw refused to say a word!

It was possible to get leave and some men went to London, which was suffering from the Blitz. One gunner was reputed to have been given a lift back to camp in a chauffeur-driven car, with an old lady in the back who turned out to be no less than Queen Mary!

In early September another invasion alert went out. The Battery Commander, Major Paul Pettit, recalls that he and other members of 'C' Battery were in the local cinema at the time. A message was flashed on to the screen for all troops to return to camp, and Major Pettit spent the rest of the night sorting out ammunition for the various types of guns they had, which included 25-pounders, 18-pounders, 4.5-inch Howitzers and even French 75-millimetres.

The Regiment went to Larkhill and had its first firing camp on 24 September 1940. Guns had to be borrowed from the Depot Regiment at Larkhill and each battery was able to have a full day's firing practice. At the time all seemed to go well, with effective fire being produced, but the reality was that the efficiency of the Regiment could be greatly improved, although everyone had tried their best.

During the next four months 'C' Battery (and 12th Regiment) was to undergo a 'sea change' in its attitudes, which was to have a lasting and beneficial effect on its fortunes.

By October 1940 the Battery had had three Battery Commanders and, as has been seen, had little equipment to train with. As if this were not enough, even more changes were to sweep through its ranks. On 1 November 1940 the Regiment moved to the Oxfordshire–Berkshire border and 'C' Battery found itself based at Wantage. In making this move, 12th Regiment became part of the 6th Armoured Division, the formation it was to fight with until the end of the war.

CHAPTER THREE

Stiffening the sinews

In peace there's nothing so becomes a man
As modest stillness and humility.
But when the blast of war blows in our ears,
Then imitate the action of the tiger;
Stiffen the sinews, summon up the blood,
Disguise fair nature by hard favoured rage.

Henry V
William Shakespeare

In November 1940 a third battery – 'F' Battery – was formed under the command of Major J. Harrington. Both 'C' and 'D' Batteries supplied cadres for this new battery and then lost another 45 officers and men to help form a new HAC regiment, named 13th (HAC) Regiment RHA. It became necessary for 12th Regiment to receive a considerable number of replacements: the incoming draft amounted to 293 ORs, of whom 130 were from the Royal Scots and 16 from the Argyll and Sutherland Highlanders. Although these men had trained only as infantrymen, they proved to be excellent material for training as Horse Artillery gunners.

It was also in November 1940 that Lt Colonel G.R.N. Heseltine MC RHA handed over the command of 12th Regiment to Lt Colonel P.L. Graham MC RHA. It was probably a timely transfer of command for Lt Colonel Heseltine had endeared himself to everyone.

> He made it his business to know all his men as well, if not better, than their own troop subalterns. It was this spirit of friendliness among all personnel in the Regiment which was to become the foundation of the Regimental spirit, which could have few equals in any regiment in the British Army.[1]

The new Commanding Officer, known as 'Ludo' (his Christian names were Patrick Ludovic), was tall, slim and handsome, with iron-grey hair and moustache. The impact he had on 12th Regiment is well explained in his obituary, written by Lt Colonel J.A.T. Barstow DSO TD, which appeared in the HAC *Journal* in August 1958. Colonel Graham had been killed during the sacking of the British Embassy in Baghdad earlier that year.

> He found a Regt. containing first class material in officers and men and great enthusiasm but lacking in technical knowledge. This he proceeded to impart with the greatest energy and every officer and man who later served in action in North Africa and Italy will testify to the tremendous value of the training received from him.
>
> 'Ludo' Graham was one of the Regular Officers who, after the First War in which he had won the MC as a subaltern in a Horse Artillery battery, devoted his very considerable brain and enthusiasm to the study of his profession and in his case to the techniques and tactics of Gunnery. The H.A.C has been particularly fortunate in having over the years had contact with and training from so many of this comparatively small band.
>
> 'Ludo' was a Horse Artilleryman in every sense of the word. He insisted always on the highest standards of technical skill, behaviour and turnout. If he himself could not supply the expertise – and there were very few branches in which he was not himself exceedingly competent – he saw to it that others could provide first class instruction. He was a firm believer in the axiom that if the Officers are good

at their job the unit will be all right, and he harried his officers with unrelenting energy and caustic tongue. One remembers well the long Exercises in all conditions, the innumerable TEWTs, his insistence on rigid March Discipline, meticulous Accuracy, constant checks and counterchecks, Speed everywhere, Dispersion and Camouflage all the time, and also the more individual idiosyncrasies. The slogans 'It's speed that kills' – 'Mental Alertness' – 'Basic Polish' – no one knew what the latter was except that no officer ever had enough of it to satisfy him! But the abiding memory is of respect for the realism and imagination which characterised all his training and the conviction that it saved many lives in action later.

His energy and enthusiasm evoked a ready response in most of his subordinates, and those who failed to come up to his standards, Regular or Territorial alike, were ruthlessly eliminated.

In the process a few good ones were lost but in retrospect one must admit that the Regiment and the Company probably gained from the drastic methods employed *pour encourager les autres*.

As well as the intensive training of his Regt., 'Ludo' took a passionate interest in the Tactical Handling of Artillery and especially in the role of Artillery in Support of Armoured Formations. His teaching on these subjects was brilliant and probably much in advance of his time. One can only say that almost everything he foretold and advised came to be proved correct in the actual battle.

In December 1940 another personality arrived to influence the progress of 'C' Battery: Major Clive Usher RHA, who took over command of the Battery from Major Paul Pettit. Like Colonel Graham, Major Usher was a regular officer with an equal passion for attaining the highest standards which are the hallmark of the Royal Horse Artillery. He had a strong, good-looking, rather craggy face, with a determined mouth and jaw and a hooked nose. His strong, lively personality meant that he was constantly on the go. He was physically hard and fit. The story goes that as a subaltern he used to go around the fair grounds fighting the local professionals in the boxing booths, and he usually won! He was a natural and fearless leader of men who, realizing that he would always give a hundred per cent of himself for them, responded with loyalty, enthusiasm and affection. He was to turn 'C' Battery into a very formidable weapon of war.

Another, albeit rather more distant, officer who also had an influence on 'C' Battery's performance was Brigadier T. Lyon-Smith, nicknamed 'Tiger'. He was the officer commanding the Support Group in 6th Armoured Division, of which 12th Regiment was then a part. He was a direct and outspoken character who believed in getting out and about with the batteries under his command. On many occasions on an exercise the cry would go up from a gun position, 'Look out, Tiger's about!'

Thus it was that in 1941 'C' Battery was at last able to settle down under strong and dedicated leaders to train properly for the battles which they knew

Lt Colonel Clive Usher DSO, *described after the war as being 'the father of 'C' Battery', commanded 'C' Battery from January 1941 to March 1942. This picture was taken just before he became* CRA *of 6th Armoured Division in Italy in 1944. Note the battle-axe badge of 78th Division on his battle-dress.*

were to come. Although there were the inevitable changes of personnel during the next five years, the large proportion of the Battery were together for that period.

In retrospect, it would seem that there had been adequate time for training during the following 22 months but in fact, at the time, the Regiment was never sure when it would be required to be ready for active service and so was unable to think more than three or four months ahead.

The tempo of training increased and firing camps and exercises followed in quick succession, as the War Diary[2] shows:

1941

Feb 23	Week's Practice camp at West Down.
March 3	'C' Battery moved to Chatteris (near Huntingdon, Cambridgeshire).
March 6	'C' Battery comprised of a troop of 25 pdrs and a troop of 18 pdrs.
March 30	The whole Regiment equipped with 24 x 25 pounders.
April 27	'C' Battery under canvas at Hinxton Grange, Operation Thunderbolt.
June 29	En route to Larkhill, 12th Regiment harboured at Hungerford and spent the day playing football and cricket with 11th (HAC) Regt RHA whom they were next to see in Tunisia nearly two years later.
June 30	West Down, Knighton & Larkhill ranges, one day's firing practice.
July 2	Operation 'Bulldog' at Stamford. 6th Armoured Division exercise.
July 25–27	Anti-tank shooting at Foulness.
August 31–Sept 4	Practice camp at Larkhill.
Sept 9	6th Armoured Division inspected by His Majesty the King, the Captain General at Lakenheath in Norfolk.
Sept 27–Oct 3	Exercise Bumper – daily changes of position between Bury St Edmunds in Suffolk and Woburn in Buckinghamshire.
November 9–13	Sennybridge – Firing Camp.

Although they required a great deal of effort and often entailed very little sleep, most exercises are unmemorable in retrospect. However, there was one exercise in which not only 12th Regiment took part but the whole of 6th Armoured Division; indeed, it was the largest exercise of its kind in the history of the British Army. This was Exercise Bumper, which took place between 27 September and 3 October 1941. It involved an Army Group of two corps defending central and southern England being attacked from the east by an Army Group of similar size. The exercise was directed by General Alan Brooke with General Bernard Montgomery acting as chief umpire. At battery and regimental level, it meant taking up positions between Bury St Edmunds and Woburn.

The results of the post mortem were far reaching because the exercise had revealed a can of worms from a gunnery point of view. This showed a faulty overall command structure, which led to a complete shambles.

It is beyond the limits of this history to discuss these lofty matters, but the interested reader is recommended to read Brigadier Shelford Bidwell's book *Gunners at War*, in which he comments that not only was the command structure at fault but of much more relevance to 'C' Battery and 12th Regiment there had been a

general failure to provide effective artillery support in the shape of planned and organized fire. As has been said, the guiding principle for any artilleryman, whether he is supporting a company or a corps, is that the infantry must never be allowed to go into the attack without carefully planned covering fire from every available gun based on the best available information about the enemy. Here, in a situation where the new armies were imagined facing the conquerors of Europe and half Russia, the infantry were continually allowed to attack naked of support other than by observation on 'targets of opportunity' which, in artillery terms, is locking the stable door after the horse has bolted. It was not good enough to argue that the pace of modern operations precluded fire-planning. The greater the mobility the greater the need for artillery fire to be both anticipatory and prophylactic. If the artillery techniques were too slow then they would have to be made faster.[3]

'C' Battery lined up on parade for an inspection by King George VI at Lakenheath, Norfolk, as part of 6th Armoured Division on 9 September 1941.

Those responsible for these matters saw that the command structure was sorted out. The problem of providing fast and accurate fire support was partly the tech-

nical problem of radio communication and partly a tactical one of organization. It was providential that wirelesses were being developed to meet the demands of the situation. Originally, only one wireless operator could speak to another one but, by using different wave lengths, units began to circulate information to several stations at once. No. 19 sets were not easy to operate and it required much practice and strict signals discipline to make the system work. A battery would have both troop commanders, the Battery Captain and the Battery Commander equipped with wirelesses, to act as observation posts.

It was now possible for troop commanders to obtain immediate fire of their own battery, i.e. eight guns, and through the Battery Commander the fire of flanking batteries, as likely as not those of their own regiment; and ultimately and very important, the fire of every gun within range. This meant that the entire artillery of a division, a corps or even an army could be obtained within a very short period of time. It was estimated that it took nearly an hour to fire a divisional target using old procedures but now, by using better communications, a divisional target could be hit within five minutes of the original order.

> The system came into being without any specific name except the letters of the phonetic alphabet 'Uncle' for 'U', which was a demand for the whole divisional artillery, and 'Mike' for 'M', for the whole regiment. There was always an air of emergency and trying to beat the clock about them. The opening call, an urgent, thrice-repeated cry of 'Uncle Target! Uncle Target! Uncle Target!' screamed into the microphone of a No. 19 radio set, in that nasal tenor or soprano voice affected by all the best operators, would galvanize the entire artillery net, waking up duty officers, demanding the straining attention of signallers and gun position officers for the next order and sending detachments running to their posts in action. It was always intensely dramatic and, even at practice, the phonetic 'Uncle' was highly charged and there was always intense eagerness and competition to be the first battery ready to engage.[4]

Thus it is seen that 'C' Battery played a small part in the development of the history of British gunnery. It will also be seen later on how 12th Regiment called for and got the first 'Uncle Target' of the war and later in Italy how a troop commander of 'C' Battery called for and got an 'Uncle Target' of his own.

During the first three months of 1942 the Battery stayed at Shelford and carried out individual training. A lot of this was of a distinctly physical nature. Major Clive Usher's famous weekly cross-country runs were a case in point. These runs were several miles long and much to the frustration of all concerned, Clive Usher, with his dog Bash running at his heel, always arrived back first, regularly beating officers and men who fancied themselves as runners. The Battery Commander would then time everyone home and woe betide the officer who arrived more than a minute or two behind him!

Colonel 'Ludo' Graham was particularly keen on physical fitness as well and on the coldest mornings of the winter would not allow any officer or man to wear balaclava headwear and scarves in open vehicles, which was a real hardship.

On another occasion Colonel Graham addressed 'C' Battery in a howling gale, which blew his words into his face, and realizing he couldn't be heard he called out to Major Usher, 'Turn the Battery round Clive, I can't talk into this wind.' The Battery was consequently marched round to the other side of Colonel Graham, whereupon he turned round himself and continued talking with the wind behind him.

This order became quite a catch phrase in the Battery, and three years later in Italy Gunner Thomas recalled, 'A pitch black night in Italy, when the wind was howling, the rain was slashing and the guns were crashing, when the very miserable voice of Dennis Smyth came from under a ground sheet, "Turn the Battery round Clive, we can't talk into this wind". It was very funny at a time when there wasn't a lot to laugh at.'[5]

Then, of course, there were games of soccer, rugby and that most martial sport, boxing. There were inter-battery and inter-unit bouts. After one such contest, the Commanding Officer of the Support Group, Brigadier 'Tiger' Lyon-Smith was so impressed that he wrote the following letter of appreciation to Colonel 'Ludo' Graham:

> I want to congratulate your Regiment on the grand team you put into the boxing tournament. I thought they were all first rate and never have I seen men go into the ring more determined to knock hell out of their opponents! Every single man went 'all out' from the word go and they couldn't have fought *harder* and *cleaner*…
>
> I congratulate the team and all those who assisted in organisation and training. I have never felt any fear of the Regiment, or any part of it, ever letting the Regiment down, or failing to do their best. This success shows once again that we have the spirit and determination to win anything. To this spirit we have only to add, and even improve upon, the individual skill and collective efficiency.[6]

Three weeks before this boxing match, Major Clive Usher left the Battery to take over command of 138 Field Regiment RA. This was only one step in his highly successful wartime service, in which he was to finish as a Brigadier with a DSO and bar and the CRA of 6th Armoured Division. He had made a massive contribution to the training of 'C' Battery during his time as Battery Commander over the 14-month period and he left it an extremely efficient unit, well able to fight 'the most professionally skilful army of modern times' – Hitler's *Wehrmacht*. Major Usher handed over command of the Battery to Major J.F. Wilson, who held this position for only two months, after which he was forced to give up because of illness.

On 11 April 1942 the Regiment moved from Shelford to Builth Wells in South Wales, a distance of 204 miles, without any major breakdowns. There they attended a firing camp, consisting of battery and regimental schemes, after which they drove 326 miles to Dam Park Camp, Ayr, in Scotland, also without mishap. The camp was under canvas by the river Doon. Training continued during a wet summer.

On 22 April the Regiment practised loading vehicles and equipment on to Royal Navy Tank landing craft. Other exercises placed emphasis on working with and getting to know other units in 6th Armoured Division. Exercises Shuyt, Stymie and Fist took place during the months of May, June and July, and 'C' Battery had its own particular days with 16th/5th Lancers, Lothian and Border Horse and 17th/21st Lancers. Much time was also spent on practice with small arms, both on the ranges and on the beach at Ayr. The War Diary records show that on 16 July 550 men of the regiment classified in Musketry.

It was clear to everyone that with emphasis on divisional training and practice with shipping, the Regiment might be going to war before long.

On 15 May Major James Grose took over command of 'C' Battery. Fair-haired and good-looking, Major Grose proved to be a highly competent battery commander and won the respect of everyone.

In August, the Regiment took part in its last big exercise – Dry Shod. Ironically, it poured with rain throughout. The idea of the exercise was to study the crossing of the Channel and striking inland from a beach-head. All those involved were totally exhausted after six days and nights of trying to cope with the elements and their tactical requirements. There was little doubt that this exercise and others were as near as possible to the realities of war as could be obtained without the danger of enemy fire. It will be seen how this training stood 'C' Battery and the Regiment in good stead in the years to come.

On 24 August Lt Colonel 'Ludo' Graham relinquished command of the Regiment. It must have been a great disappointment to him personally that he was not allowed to lead 12th Regiment into battle. He had dedicated himself to preparing it for war, with conspicuous success. He was succeeded by Lt Colonel G.W. Mansell RHA, who on 30 August addressed the Regiment on parade, informing them that they, as part of 6th Armoured Division, were due to proceed abroad in an easterly direction. Leave was to be completed by 13 September and all vehicles were to be painted light brown, but no issue of tropical kit was to be made. There was considerable excitement at this announcement and speculation on where the Battery would be sent. The clues afforded by the type of clothing and vehicle camouflage were a source of considerable debate.

'C' Battery were told to be in readiness to embark from Port 'A' on 6 September. Divisional signs on vehicles were washed over with distemper and badges on battle dress were removed. Although it looked as if the Battery were soon to be on the high seas, it was another six weeks before they embarked.

At the end of September the Regiment listened to a lecture by Brigadier H.B. Latham RHA on German tactics in the Middle East, which was followed by an inspection of German tanks. On 29 September 'C' Battery's guns and vehicles were driven to Liverpool docks and loaded on board two ships. Each ship carried the tanks, guns and vehicles of various armoured, infantry and artillery units.

On 15 October the Regiment was inspected by the Captain General HM The King and finally 'C' Battery was ordered to go to a port on the Clyde to embark for an unknown destination. It was to sail as part of a force of mixed arms in advance of the rest of the Regiment.

The Battery entrained at Ayr and much to their disgust found themselves locked into their compartments by the Military Police. 'X' Troop and one half of Battery Headquarters embarked on the SS *Arundel Castle* and 'W' Troop, with the remainder of the Battery, embarked on the SS *Cameronia*. On 1 November 1942 they set sail. Mike Austin-Smith wrote in a letter of 13 November 1943:

> The long line of large ships weighed anchor and in line astern passed majestically through the boom and steamed silently and very slowly down the Firth. Little tugs with their crews cheering us slipped by, an incoming submarine flashed 'God Speed' and all the while we were gliding smoothly past familiar landscapes growing dim in the fading light. Soon the land became just a black mass with a few twinkling lights and the ships ahead just little blobs on the cold black sea. The darkness came quickly obliterating everything, land was too distant to see any light and the ships showed not even a navigation light.
>
> The ship began to rise and fall very slightly and we knew England was behind and that we were upon the ocean, outward bound.

After three and a half years 'C' Battery was on the way to war.

'C' BATTERY 12th (HAC) REGIMENT RHA

Order of Battle 29 October 1942

Battery Commander		Major J.E. Grose
Battery Captain		Captain S.N. Rae
CPO		Lt K. Hunt
CPO/A		Lt T.N.W. Lacey

	W TROOP		X TROOP
Troop Commander	Captain A.G.P. Lincoln		Captain H.G.St G. Pollock
GPO	Lt H.E. Chubb		Lt E.A. Forestier-Walker
Troop Leader	Lt I.G. Miller		Lt H.N. Atherton
BSM/TSM	BSM M.L. George	BSM W. Pearston	BSM R. Mackenzie
BQMS		BQMS W.F. Collen-Jones	
No. 1s	Sgt T.W. Summers		Sgt R. Davis
	Sgt W.H. Fletcher		Sgt T.E. Elwick
	Sgt L.J. Westcombe		Sgt J.E. Derricott
			L/Sgt J. McAndrew
Battery Staff		Sgt J. Ashpole	
		Sgt C.A.Phillips	
		L/Sgt A. Hudspith (CPO/A)	
		Sgt W.E. Bryant (MT)	
		Sgt Marchant	
OPA	L/Sgt G.A. Ferrari		Bdr R.H. Newell

27

CHAPTER FOUR

Blade Force

We've sung the song so many times …
'They say there's a troopship just leaving Bombay …'
But now there's a troopship just leaving the Clyde
And we are on our way!

It's like walking round a city!
What keeps this thing afloat?
There's a sharp end and a blunt end
And you call it a ship, not a boat.

She's known as the Drunken Duchess
Due to the way that she rolls,
Soon her creaks and vibrations are rivalled
By the moans of suffering souls.

Meals are served but twice a day
On first or second sitting.
We also queue for booster jabs
With a needle used for knitting!

So this is the North Atlantic?
This heaving, grey green terror?
Someone up there doesn't like me,
I'm sure I've been posted in error!

Troopship
Ted Lane

As the ss *Arundel Castle* and ss *Cameronia* sailed down the Clyde, the men sorted themselves out and found that the two-tier bunks they were allotted were not uncomfortable. One of the pleasant surprises of life on board was being able to eat proper white bread again and to find the rations supplemented with tinned food from the USA.

Detachments were told to man the ship's guns, which, although they were only 12-pounders, made a much louder bang than a 25-pounder. It was agreed that the Gunner's Mate probably knew what he was talking about when he told the gun crews to wear earplugs! However, uppermost in everyone's mind were thoughts of their unknown destination.

At this stage it is pertinent to consider the general situation of the war at that moment. The war between Germany and Britain and France only became a 'world war' when Germany invaded Russia and Japan treacherously attacked the outposts of the United States in the Pacific, and Germany gratuitously declared war on the United States. Italy's declaration of war became a direct threat to Britain's position on the Mediterranean through which ran the vital communications to India. At the same time the collapse of the Soviet armies allowed the Germans to threaten Persia and the Middle East on which Britain depended for her supplies of oil.

There followed a long and acrimonious debate between the Allies on the correct strategy to be followed. The Russians demanded a 'second front', in North West Europe, to relieve the pressure on their own fronts, at once.

The Americans, faced with a two-front war, with great wisdom, decided to give the defeat of Germany the first priority, proposing to launch an army across the Channel into occupied France in 1942 or, at the latest, in 1943.

The British, also faced with a two-front war (the other in South-East Asia), were in a difficult position, being the weakest member of the allied team, depending on the US for vital equipment, but with much experience in fighting the formidable Germans.

It would take a long time to equip, organize and train an Anglo–American force to attempt so hazardous an operation as a landing on the fortified Channel coast. The British preferred a Mediterranean strategy, but since it was politically impossible to do nothing until 1944, they persuaded the reluctant Americans to make a joint invasion of French North Africa in 1942. The aim was to establish bases in Algeria and Tunisia and, advancing eastwards as rapidly as possible, capture Tunis and crush the Axis forces between the First and the Eighth Armies.

The political situation in French North Africa was too complicated to explain briefly here, but the Anglo–American partners hoped that bold action would rally at least part of the French forces to the Allied cause before the Germans could react and organize a front facing west.

This proved a vain hope and much hard fighting lay ahead until Axis resistance collapsed in May 1943. The force committed to Torch, the landings in North Africa was placed under General Dwight D. Eisenhower, its land element comprising an American and British Corps and later a Free French contingent.

The boldest and perhaps over-ambitious part of the Allied plan was to despatch a small mobile battle-group entitled 'Blade Force' in a dash to seize Tunis, the vital Axis port of entry. This was to be 'C' Battery's entry into active operations. Its composition was:

17th/21st Lancers
'C' Battery 12th HAC Regt RHA (25-pounders)
'B' Sqn 1st Derbyshire Yeomanry (armoured cars)
'A' Battery 72nd Anti-tank Regt RA (6-pounders)
'C' Troop 51st Light AA Regt RA (Bofors)
Troop 5th Field Sqn RE
'B' Company 10th Rifle Brigade (Motor Company)
2 Sections 165th Light Field Ambulance

It was only on 5 November when their ships were far out in the Atlantic, that sealed orders were opened and 'C' Battery learnt of these plans and the historic part they were selected to play in them. They were to form part of the armoured Regimental Combat Group mentioned above. This group was to be under the command of Colonel R.A. Hull (who had recently commanded the 17th/21st Lancers) and would be considered part of the 78th Division, which had been formed only five months previously. This Division's badge was a battle axe and 'C' Battery's armoured Regimental Combat Group was perceived as the cutting edge of the advance on Tunis; thus it was named Blade Force.

Writing nearly 50 years after the event, it is easy to forget or discredit the unknown dangers that existed at that time. Operation Torch was astonishingly daring and successful. The enormous armada of ships, a large proportion of which had sailed across the Atlantic, were combined in the greatest amphibious operation in history at that time. Furthermore, it comprised Americans and British, who were fighting in the war together for the first time on land. They had no idea how the French would react to their invasion. There were, in fact, eight poorly equipped French divisions backed by 500 aircraft in French North Africa. There was no great love for the Allies in their ranks, and especially not for the British after the attacks on their fleets at Oran and Dakar which had taken place in 1940 and had been so stoutly resisted.[1]

Nor was the reaction of the French the only worry. It was possible that the Allies would have great difficulty in arriving at their destinations without suffering heavy losses at sea. The period from August 1942 to May 1943 was the worst of the war for Allied shipping losses from German U-boats. In fact, the month of the invasion, November 1942, was to prove the peak of shipping tonnage sunk by U-boats in the whole war (729,000 tons).[2] And yet, on the outward journey, only one of the 111 transports involved in Torch was sunk by a submarine.

The size of the naval escort also was colossal: 216 warships in all sailed to protect the precious merchantmen and troopships. The first convoy to Algiers, consisting of 35 transports, was escorted by 51 warships of all sizes with a further fleet, Force H, consisting of 3 battleships and 3 aircraft carriers, which steamed before them. If this seems excessive, it should be remembered that only three months previously, between 11 and 12 August 1942, a convoy of 14 merchantmen bound for Malta from Gibraltar required an escort of 2 battleships, 3 aircraft carriers, 7 cruisers and 32 destroyers. Despite this massive protection, only 3 merchantmen arrived in one piece, together with 2 others who crawled into Malta in a sinking condition; that is to say, nearly two-thirds of the convoy was sunk. Nor did the escort force get off lightly: 1 carrier was sunk and the 2 others were damaged, along with 2 cruisers and 2 destroyers sunk and 2 cruisers damaged. The hazards of sailing in the Mediterranean were considerable: added to the efforts of the Axis navies and air forces, further speculation arose about what the considerable French fleet[3] basically stationed at Toulon might do. Above all, no one on the Allied side knew if the enemy knew they were coming. Amazingly, they did not, and so when the good ships *Arundel Castle* and *Cameronia* sailed through the Straits of Gibraltar on the night of 11 November, the landings had been successfully made at all three objectives two days earlier and patchy resistance by the French was nearly over.[4] Complete surprise had been achieved.

Meanwhile, 'C' Battery lined the rails of their ships and gaped in amazement at the lights of Tangier on the starboard bow and in awe at the dark blackened shape of the Rock on the port side.

On 12 November they sailed into a sunlit Algiers harbour and disembarked during that day and the next. Algiers was a splendid sight of cream and white buildings crowding the hills around the harbour, offset by green trees and a vivid blue sky. All was hustle and bustle, with Frenchmen, Arabs and – for many their first such sight – Black (Senegalese) soldiers as well, all going about their business. In addition to these visual impressions was the unforgettable odour of Africa – a compound of earth, dust, heat, strange scents blown across the desert and more recognizable smells, some of them not so pleasant. 'It smelt,' thought Lance Bombardier Allan Lewis perceptively, as he heaved his kit bag ashore, 'different from Europe.'

The Battery camped at the Jardin d'Essai with the rest of Blade Force. Arriving shortly before sunset, they settled down as best they could, their slumbers disturbed by the roars of lions and other animals in the nearby zoo. Next morning, the fatigue party who had dug a latrine found they had made a tactical error – they had placed it in the middle of a cactus bed!

That day, Blade Force received orders to move to Tunis as soon as possible. The Force was split into two halves: the first half, consisting of the 'B' Company 10th Rifle Brigade, Armoured Cars and Force HQ, were to travel by road to meet up with 'C' Squadron 17th/21st Lancers, who would proceed by rail. The second half, consisting of the rest of the Force including 'C' Battery, were to follow up as quickly as they could and get their equipment unloaded from the ships. In fact, such were the problems caused by the constant breaking down of cranes that only 'W' Troop was able to move off with the second column, despite the best efforts of Major Grose and Captain Rae.

So 'W' Troop and Battery HQ left Algiers on Monday 16 November and marched 290 miles during the next three days to Constantine. The journey started in hot bright sunshine and the convoy passed orange groves and vineyards before it started to climb the mountains, catching an occasional glimpse of the Mediterranean sea in the distance, looking as blue as any tourist postcard. These mountains are part of the Atlas range which stretches across the length of French North Africa from Morocco to Tunisia. They vary in height from 500 feet to over 6000 feet; they are often steep and craggy, with pine, cork and olive trees and cactus groves at the bottom and scrub grass or bare rock at the top. The Arab name for a mountain is a *Djebel*. The road climbed and wound over and through the mountains, seldom wide enough to allow two lorries to pass. As their journey continued the weather deteriorated, bringing rain, snow and frost at night. At last, the column managed to arrive at Constantine in sunlight and everyone was impressed by this ancient city, with its white houses and blocks of apartments built on the edge of a gorge spanned by a great viaduct.

It was during the journey to Constantine that the Battery suffered its first fatal casualty while on active service. Gunner G.P. Bright was severely injured and subsequently died following a road accident involving the Battery's water wagon. The next day (20 November) the column marched another 130 miles to Souk-Ahras and harboured in a very muddy racecourse for the night.

At this stage the reader is advised to look at the map on the front endpaper. The Atlas mountains straggle and roll across Algeria into Tunisia and finally come to an end in a coastal plain which is narrow in the north but spreads out in the south. But there is no regularity in this geography. The features to look for are the valleys, which are avenues of advance, and the mountains and hills on either side, which are the cornerstones of defence. It is good country to defend and hence infantry rather than tanks is required to take possession of the vital high ground.

On the coast in the north is Bizerta, the nearest port to Sicily and used by the Germans to unload ships carrying men, weapons and equipment. A railway line runs south to a junction at Mateur, where one line thrusts due west through the mountains towards the coast, passing Green and Bald Hills outside Jefna, and on to Sedjenane and Djebel Abiod; another line makes its way through the mountains in a south-westerly direction, passing the little station of Sidi Nsir and going on to Beja, Souk-el-Arba and finally Algiers, nearly 500 miles away. A third railway line from Mateur loops round in an easterly direction to connect with a line which follows the River Medjerda from south of Beja to emerge at Djedeida on the way to Tunis; the small town of Tebourba will be seen at a gap in the hills and at the head of the valley down which the River Medjerda meanders from Medjez-el-Bab, meaning 'the key of the gate'. About six miles north of Medjez-el-Bab is a sinister and foreboding hill not a thousand feet high, named Longstop by the British.

Twenty miles south of Medjez another railway line emerges on the way to Tunis, passing through Bou Arada and going on to the more open country at Pont du Fahs. Still going south, the mountains close in again; south of Robaa they separate like a forked tail, the Eastern Dorsal struggling south with passes at Fondouk, Faid and finally Gafsa. The Western Dorsal is pierced by passes at Sbiba, Thala and Kasserine.

Already elements of 78th Division were discovering the hard way how difficult it was to make progress against a skilful enemy in mountainous country. The small port of Bone had been captured by commandos and two companies of 3rd Bn Parachute Regiment on 13 November. This had allowed the 6th Bn Royal West Kents to land at the port from two destroyers, and they all advanced along the road leading to Bizerta. On 17 November they were held up by a force of German tanks at Djebel Abiod and were not strong enough to advance further.

This action had already been fought by the time 'W' Troop were ordered to proceed to Souk-el-Arba on 20 November. But the column had not been on the road for long before it was directed to Teboursouk 80 miles away, which it reached at midday, and here the Troop went into action in support of some French troops who, although poorly equipped, were rallying to the Allied cause. No shots being fired, the Troop advanced 12 miles to Testour where Captain Aubrey Lincoln installed his OP at the top of a minaret. They were dive-bombed here by Stukas but suffered no casualties.

On Sunday 22 November the Troop moved first of all to Le Kef, then to Souk-el-Arba where it met up with 'X' Troop who had finally arrived from Algiers. Souk-el-Arba had a railway station and an airfield, and had been taken by 1st Bn Parachute Regiment in a parachute landing on 15 November. By the time 'C' Battery concentrated there two squadrons of Spitfires were operating from the airfield, but heavy rainfall was turning the airstrip into a quagmire and it became impossible for the aircraft to use it after a day or so. Rain was not the only thing that was falling from the heavens – German bombers operating from all-weather airfields near Tunis were making repeated bombing raids over the area. On one occasion a fuel dump exploded in a huge ball of fire and Spitfires were seen diving on enemy aircraft. They were unable to inflict any damage because they had run out of ammunition.

There were other shortages that were beginning to frustrate the advance of the Allied forces. By now nearly 450 miles separated them from Algiers and the railway system was woefully inadequate to cope with the massive amount of supplies needed to sustain 78th Division's progress. They halted for two days to build up some stocks of food, fuel and ammunition, while the Army Commander told London how 'woefully weak' his forces were to sustain an advance on Tunis.

Nevertheless, the order to advance was given two days later, on 23 November, and a three-pronged attack was set in motion. On the northern route 36th Brigade was to advance through the passes to Jefna and then it was to swing right towards Mateur. Blade Force, with the only armour available (17th/21st Lancers were to be joined by 1st Battalion 1st US Armored Regiment) was to advance via Beja to Mateur. On the southern flank, 11th Brigade was to attack Medjez-el-Bab and advance up the valley of the River Medjerda to Tebourba and Djedeida.

On Tuesday 24 November the Battery moved up to Beja in the late afternoon. By this time the extent of the enemy's air superiority became increasingly apparent. The further the Allies advanced the further they were from their own air forces, who had an increasingly difficult task to operate because of the distance from their airfields and because they could not use all-weather runways. Only Bone had runways which could cope with the rapidly deteriorating weather conditions to any extent, and Bone was 100 miles away, whereas the Luftwaffe had only to fly about 40 miles from their all-weather airfields outside Tunis. The Battery Commander became the first, albeit slight, casualty, wounded in the leg from the fire of a Junkers 88.

The next day, 25 November, saw Blade Force advancing in three columns: wheeled traffic on the left flank went up the road to Sidi Nsir Station, 17th/21st Lancers with the Rifle Brigade moved on a centre line cross-country towards Mateur, and 1st Battalion 1st US Armored Regiment moved in parallel on the right flank. The road to Sidi Nsir was strafed all day and at about 1430 hours Lance Bombardier Keddie was killed during an attack by eight JU 88s. This tragedy was made no less poignant by the fact that he had been married on his embarkation leave a month earlier.

Meanwhile, the centre column had advanced on this bright sunny morning and at 1300 hours one of the leading armoured cars of 'B' Squadron 1st Derbyshire Yeomanry was fired on as it approached a T-junction about six miles south of Mateur. About 600 yards up the road to Mateur were two farms on either side of the road. The fire had come from a gun in the left-hand farm. The Company Commander of 'B' Company 10th Rifle Brigade, Major Elkington, held an 'O' Group which Captain Aubrey Lincoln, leading 'W' Troop, had a lot of trouble reaching because his carrier was immobilized by mud which had balled up into its tracks. Two platoon commanders of the Rifle Brigade had sim-

Captain Aubrey Lincoln commanded 'W' Troop during the fighting in Tunisia until April 1943. He subsequently commanded 'B' Battery, The Ayrshire Yeomanry, 152 Field Regiment RA in Italy, where he was awarded the Military Cross. After the war he commanded 'C' Battery from 1947 to 1951.

ilar trouble with their motorbikes and, in the end, all of them had to climb on to a couple of scout cars to go forward.

The battle plan was that 'C' Squadron 17th/21st Lancers would attack first the right-hand farm and then the left-hand farm. The Rifle Brigade was to send in platoons to support both of these attacks, 'W' Troop was to fire on both farms, which were also to be softened up by the machine-guns of the armoured cars.

Captain Lincoln's carrier at last managed to crawl up to within 300 yards of his position, and then broke down again. However, since he could observe properly from his carrier he went back to it. He recalled the remainder of the action in a letter home:

> I started ranging – I was so excited at firing my first shot in action (incidentally the first to be fired in the regiment) that I used the wrong scale to measure the range and the first two rounds went miles over. I didn't see them, but they probably got some Hun cooks or quartermasters! I realised the mistake and measured again and by wonderful luck (as at that time we only had very small scale maps) the next round landed right in the hedge surrounding the farm. The infantry thought it was wonderful! We always pretend it's very difficult, to impress them!
>
> By this time the carriers were up to the farm, as there was practically no

resistance there. They were mostly Italians and showed the white flag early, asking for medical help as they said they had a lot of casualties from the machine-gunning. They hadn't – they were just Italians! So I moved the fire on to the left-hand farm and had some fun firing at the gun which was firing at the road near us. I could see its flash. It turned out afterwards to be a tank, and although my fire kept it moving about a bit, it didn't do much harm.

The left-hand party were now moving. One of the carriers with them hit a mine, and shortly afterwards they were held up by machine-gun fire, having got pretty close to their objective. The situation was soon relieved by our tanks which moved in behind, having cleared up the right-hand farm – and these chaps, mostly Germans, also surrendered.

The position was consolidated, and our thoughts turned to food – it was now afternoon and we'd had nothing since our rather scanty breakfast.

About 120 prisoners were brought in, and at dusk they were marched back to our gun position, much to the delight of my men. They spent the night there being guarded by our chaps and some of the armoured cars whose lights were kept on them all night.

Lt Anthony Naumann, the commander of the platoon that attacked the left-hand farm, wrote in an article in *Blackwoods Magazine* in July 1943:

> We waited for the artillery. Suddenly a little cloud of smoke seemed to rise lazily from the ground, and a second or so later we heard the crack of the shell as it went off. The guns were shooting beautifully, scoring a direct hit on the buildings and pitching their shells in the target area.

During this attack Lt Naumann was wounded in the head and arm by machine-gun fire and lost his sight, and a number of his men lost their lives.

On the following day, 26 November, 'W' Troop was once again in action supporting 17th/21st Lancers who, together with the American tanks, successfully repulsed a German attack, knocking out 15 out of 16 German Panzers for the loss of 8 of their own tanks. The Troop was also heartened to see 2 Junkers 88s shot down by light AA fire.

It was the turn of Captain Guy Pollock's 'X' Troop to go into action on 27 November, supporting the American tanks and firing at enemy Panzers, but without clear results. 'X' Troop was again in action the next day, this time supporting 17th/21st Lancers, and had a very successful shoot on an enemy-occupied farm.

All this time the German aircraft, now flying from airfields only 20 miles away, continued to strafe the Battery at every opportunity, so that vehicle movement was restricted to after dark, if possible. The attacks were by Focke Wulfs 190s, Junkers 88s and Messerschmitt 109s, the latter often flying in pairs and quickly christened 'Mutt and Jeff'. The number of vehicles which had been shot up was rising alarmingly, with one or two men suffering wounds. One of them, Gunner Gordon Thomas, recalled what happened to him:

> At about 4 o'clock on the freezing cold morning of the 28th November, at a spot I know not where, I climbed out of my vehicle to inspect my Bren gun, when a bullet arrived from out of the blue, struck a rock by my head and, it would seem, ricocheted across my forehead and took off my steel helmet. It cut the top of my head very neatly and something, probably rock dust, went into my right eye. My face was covered in blood and there were horrified looks on the faces of my companions. The right side of my face was quite numb and someone put a large dressing over my eye. There was nothing else to be done until I could be taken to an MO.[5]

Gunner Thomas was finally patched up at a Regimental Aid Post and returned to Battery HQ.

The Battery went into action at first light on 30 November, in a position south of Chouigui, facing north. Here they supported the 17th/21st Lancers and, with Major Grose and Captain Lincoln observing, the Battery fired at a number of targets. This day was probably one of the worst for enemy air attack and the gun position was dive-bombed by Stukas (Junkers 87s fitted with sirens which wailed like demented banshees when they dived). Captain Lincoln's tank was damaged by machine-gun fire and had to be towed away in the night. During this time the situation was very fluid and no one was very clear where the enemy was, or where their own troops were either. It was possibly not surprising that the RAF also had trouble in identifying friendly forces. When Gunner Thomas, whose wound had been giving him considerable trouble, tried to get some rest in an empty pig trough at BHQ, he was roused by a burst of machine-gun fire and the sound of planes:

> I jumped up in time to see Hurricane fighters flying low over the trees. At this point 'Ivy' Hawkins came running up the field shouting and sobbing, 'Pickersgill and Voss are dead', and so they were. Both killed by a burst of what is now called 'friendly fire'.[6]

In another attack by a German bomber, Lance Bombardier Winter was killed. Because the Battery moved very shortly afterwards, his body was left behind and he was buried by the Germans. His grave was discovered by Captain Rae and Sergeant Harvey six months later.

It was increasingly obvious that the enemy was becoming stronger and his command of the air was seriously affecting the advance on Tunis. Nevertheless, 11th Infantry Brigade had advanced past Tebourba and the 5th Northamptons had tried in vain to take Djedeida. It will be recalled that when the Allies landed

Generalmajor Wolfgang Fischer. As commander of 10th Panzer Division he personally led Battle Group Hudel against 'C' Battery outside Tebourba on 1 December 1942. After this battle he was awarded the Knight's Cross with Oak Leaves. He also commanded the attacks on Grandstand Hill near Bou Arada between 18 and 20 January 1943. He died the following month together with his Chief of Staff, when they were blown up by a German mine. They were replaced by Oberst Fritz von Broich and Oberst-Leutnant Graf von Stauffenburg. The latter became famous because he planted the bomb which failed to kill Hitler on 20 July 1944. (Bundesarchiv)

at Algiers there were no German or Italian troops in Tunisia, but they had reacted with characteristic speed and urgency and had been flying in 750 men a day from Italy as well as shipping more men and equipment by sea. By the end of November the Axis forces had 15,500 fighting troops, 130 tanks, 60 field guns and 30 anti-tank guns. With this force available Field Marshal Kesselring had strongly criticized the local German commander, General Nehring, for falling back from Medjez-el-Bab so quickly, and ordered him to regain the ground he had lost.

Nehring delegated this task to the newly arrived commander of 10th Panzer Division, the energetic Generalmajor Wolfgang Fischer, who organized four battle groups. His plan was that two of these groups, Hudel and Lüder, with 20 and 40 Panzers respectively, were to destroy Blade Force by advancing through Chouigui and making for the Tebourba Gap and Tebourba itself. The third group, called Koch, after its commander who distinguished himself during the invasion of Crete, was to attack from the opposite direction, the south-east, at El Bathan. The remaining Djedeida battle group was to remain in reserve, holding Djedeida itself.

A look at the map on page 40 will show the reader how the stage was set on the morning of 1 December 1942. Blade Force was to the south of Chouigui,

Colonel James Grose MC commanded 'C' Battery from May to 1 December 1942, when he was wounded at the Battle of Tebourba, at which time he won the Military Cross. He subsequently recovered in time to take part in the invasion of Europe.

with 'C' Battery supporting 'B' Squadron 1st Derbyshire Yeomanry, 1st Bn 1st US Armored Regiment, 'A' Battery 72 Anti-Tank Regiment and 'B' Company 10th Rifle Brigade, now down to a platoon and a half. The 17th/21st Lancers were carrying out maintenance in a position covering the Tebourba Gap and 11th Brigade's HQ. The 5th Northamptons were to the west of Tebourba Gap and the East Surreys had companies deployed to the east on Djebel Maina and south of Tebourba at El Bathan. The 2nd Hampshires, who had taken over from the 5th Northamptons, found themselves overlooking Djedeida about three miles away.

Thus it was on the bright cold morning of 1 December, that the panzers of the battle groups Lüder and Hudel, the latter led by Generalmajor Fischer himself, began to advance through Chouigui towards Tebourba. As they deployed they took up their battle formations in the form of shallow V-shaped wedges, which gave every Panzer a good field of fire. The Derbyshire Yeomanry and 1st Bn 1st US Armored Regiment did their best to halt this attack but were forced

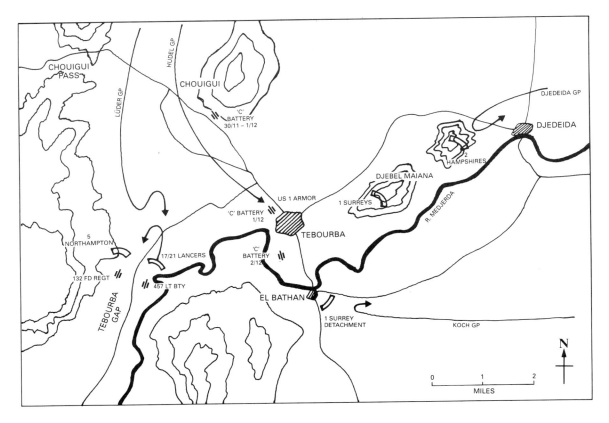

back, especially by the fire of the new long-barrelled 75mm high-velocity gun mounted on the Panzer Mark IVs. The remaining 24 Valentine and Crusader tanks of the 17th/21st Lancers now attempted to counter-attack but were themselves ambushed for their pains, losing 5 tanks before withdrawing. All this time Major Grose was able to bring down very effective fire on the German forces, supported by 25-pounders of 132nd Field Regiment Royal Artillery and 3.7-inch Howitzers of 457th Light Battery Royal Artillery, who were covering the Tebourba Gap itself. This stopped the enemy in his tracks.

At about 1300 hours Major Grose was hit in the lung but, completely disregarding his wound, continued to direct the Battery's fire. He also directed the Battery's withdrawal to a position just outside Tebourba. Although his Gunners could see the blood seeping through his shirt, he insisted on carrying on normally. He was considerably concerned whether the Battery would be able to extricate itself from its new position. Not only was the Battery engaging the enemy to the north but, because of attacks on the 2nd Hampshires to the north-east and the East Surreys to the south-east at El Bathan, rear OPs were manned by Captains Lincoln and Hunt and thus the Battery was firing almost all round the clock.

The Battle of Tebourba. The map shows Allied and German dispositions on 1 December 1942 and 'C' Battery's position on 2 December before it withdrew south. The remaining Allied forces were also forced to retire the next day after suffering heavy casualties.

All this time the Battery was also under air attack. Captain Lincoln's truck was shot up and burst into flames. Fortunately no one was killed, although his driver was wounded. All the quads were by now unserviceable or had been destroyed. Everyone was cheered, though, by the sight of the Bofors AA guns shooting down a Stuka, which crashed in flames close by. In fact, Blade Force HQ had decided that the Bofors of 'G' Troop 51st Light Anti-Aircraft Regiment RA would be best deployed protecting 'C' Battery's exposed gun positions. This anti-aircraft fire not only shot down some planes but, equally important, put off enemy aircraft from pressing home their attacks.

By the end of the day Major Grose had collapsed and was treated by an Arab doctor, there being no army doctors or ambulances available. Captain Rae took over command of the Battery, which harboured in an olive grove just south of Tebourba. A new gun position was occupied next day but there were only 20 rounds per gun left and no hope of obtaining more ammunition. The fact they had gone through an extremely tough and demanding time the day before and were so low in ammunition did not depress anyone and all were in high spirits as they breakfasted amongst the olive trees. There was special delight for those Gunners who had been able to liberate some 'goodies' in the town, such as milk chocolate, brandy and champagne. However, there was very little the Battery could do now and although Captain Rae and Lt Forestier-Walker gave the East Surreys some support by firing a few ranging rounds to bolster their morale, for the remainder of the day the guns took up anti-tank positions facing north.

In the evening, the Battery, with the battered remnants of Blade Force, was withdrawn. 'C' Battery, having no quads left, towed their guns with 8-cwt signal trucks and 3-tonners. They were ordered to harbour at Oued Zarga, about 30 miles to the south-west. On the way they were able to drop off their wounded, including Major Grose, at Medjez-el-Bab. During an arduous night drive, the new Battery Commander's truck was overturned in a bomb crater but without much harm to the passengers.

Blade Force could do no more to help and their role was taken over by the American Combat Command Group B. The hard-pressed 5th Northamptons and 1st East Surreys of 11th Brigade withdrew, having sustained heavy casualties, two days later. The 2nd Hampshires, who had fought an epic battle, did not receive the order to retire and had to split up and make for the hills.

The next day, 3 December, the Battery was able to clean itself up. After six days of frantic action they hoped to get some decent rest and sleep but were suddenly ordered, 'Prepare to move!' in order to support the remainder of Blade Force. Just as they made themselves ready, the orders were cancelled and they were able to sleep throughout the whole night with no 'stand to' the next morning. The relief was enormous.

By this time the rest of the Regiment had nearly caught up with them and so they were particularly pleased to be visited on 4 December by the CO, Lt Colonel Mansell, the 2 i/c, Major Barstow, and the padre, Captain Hearsey.

The Battery's hopes of further rest were dashed by more orders to move – not cancelled this time – and they found themselves back in the original position that they had occupied south of the T-roads 11 days before. At least this move meant that they need not do any more digging.

In this position they supported 2nd Bn Lancashire Fusiliers and 1st Bn Parachute Regiment, who were occupying the two farms that they had previously captured. Nothing happened during the next six days, except that it rained. It had rained before but not so badly as it did now, and they fought a losing battle against the mud. It was a different consistency from English mud – particularly sticky and slippery. It enveloped everything: weapons, food, clothing; even the letters the men wrote home had mud on them. Nothing except a four-wheel-drive vehicle was able to move off the roads and when it was realized that the Battery was literally sinking into its position, it took five hours to move 500 yards. Finally, on Friday 11 December, Blade Force was ordered to withdraw to Teboursouk if no action had developed by 0900 hours. But at 0800 hours, as the Battery Commander returned from his 'O' Group, sounds of gun and mortar fire could be heard as the Germans put in an attack.

Captain Lincoln, who was observing for a company of the Lancashire Fusiliers, couldn't believe his eyes when he saw a company of German infantry marching towards him in columns of three. As soon as they got into effective range, 'W' Troop's shells smashed into the column and figures could be seen running for cover; later, stretcher-bearers were seen at work. After three hours the German infantry had made their way closer to the Lancashire Fusiliers and both guns and infantry

> let rip, pinning the enemy down; some were dead, others wounded and the rest just scared stiff. Presently one of our tanks came along and frightened them still more.
>
> They ran away like hell, with everyone firing – infantry, tanks and myself, and eventually we saw what was left of them marching off the way they had come, with a few farewell rounds from our guns.

If Captain Lincoln was enjoying himself, as this extract from his aforementioned letter shows, so was Captain Hunt, who had recently taken over 'X' Troop. He was supporting the rest of the Battalion of the Lancashire Fusiliers and, like Captain Lincoln, saw a dream target of three companies of the Barenthin Regiment[7] forming up in three gullies. These gullies were exactly in the zone of 'X' Troop's guns, who rained down fire on them and caused numerous casualties. (After the campaign, Captain Hunt returned and saw the German cemetery, which was the result of his fire.) But the German attack was not stopped and Captain Hunt had to withdraw in a hurry from his exposed position with the forward platoon. He was considerably irritated to find himself under fire from a machine-gunner, who was using his valise as cover. But 'X' Troop's fire was so vigorous that the enemy could not make any more progress and, indeed, the Lancashire Fusiliers implored them to stop so that the enemy could get closer and they could have a shot at them as well. In the end the Lancashire Fusiliers and the Parachute Regiment counter-attacked with the help of a troop of 17th/21st Lancers and the enemy was well and truly seen off, losing about 100 killed, 70 prisoners and unknown wounded.

However, there was one incident that took the glister off a very successful day. As he drove a 3-tonner full of ammunition up to the gun position, BSM Pearston was shot up by an enemy machine-gun. Gunner E.M. Miles was fatally wounded and Gunner J.H. Newton was killed, but BSM Pearston drove on and delivered the ammunition safely. The enemy machine-gun was subsequently dealt with by the Paras.

This was the last action of Blade Force, which was disbanded after going out on a high note. 'C' Battery withdrew to Teboursouk to join the rest of 12th Regiment and 6th Armoured Division. 'C' Battery had fulfilled its role in Blade Force with great credit and was congratulated by the CRA Brigadier 'Tiger' Lyon-Smith, who had been given a very good report of the Battery's performance from Blade Force's commander, Colonel Hull. In the 16 days they had been in action, they had lost 6 men killed and 9 men wounded; they had fought their guns with determination, skill and courage and had learnt a great deal about their martial business. Part of their experience was the very personal one of coping with fear. Everyone remembers the first time they came under fire: everyone is frightened and feels that gut-wrenching sensation when death seems imminent. Men decorated for gallantry readily admitted that they were 'shit scared!' Good training and a strong regimental spirit, which transmits itself down to sub-unit level in the form of team spirit and comradeship, are all great antidotes to fear. But not everyone was able to cope with the 'roaring hissing menace' of enemy fire and one young officer found himself overwhelmed by this new and dreadful experience and had to be invalided back.

A final order of the day issued to all units of Blade Force by Colonel Hull stated:

> Blade did the job it was ordered to do and accounted for approximately 42 aircraft, 25 enemy armoured fighting vehicles and possibly several more, and 450 men, including prisoners. Apart from losses of vehicles by enemy action, the small number that broke down mechanically, in spite of forced marches and lack of time for maintenance, reflects very favourably on the standard of care and maintenance by drivers.

The fact that the advance on Tunis had not been successful was certainly no disgrace for the troops involved. The enemy had reacted with commendable speed and vigour and, having considerable air superiority, they had just been able to frustrate the embryonic 1st Army's best efforts; efforts made harder by having to operate at the end of an extremely tenuous 500-mile line of communications, coupled with appalling weather. Although they did not capture Tunis, they had established themselves 100 miles further east than had been originally envisaged. Certainly 'C' Battery played its part effectively and no more so than its Battery Commander, Major James Grose, who was awarded the Military Cross for his leadership and courage. His citation is quoted below.

> This officer, whilst commanding 'C' Battery 12th RHA south of Chouigui on the 1st December 1942, maintained his Battery in action against heavy tank, infantry and air attack.
>
> Although wounded, he continued to command his battery and, on receipt of orders to withdraw, successfully extricated all his guns and covered the withdrawal of our own forward troops, continuing to direct very effective fire and refusing to be evacuated until he collapsed.

CHAPTER FIVE

Tunisian victory

Haven't you heard?

The Division is harbouring here, I think,
I heard it on the R.T. link.
The lines are laid
The Latrines arranged
'But haven't you heard?
Its all been changed!'

Chorus:
Weather fine
Tracks improving
All informed
Ack.

Mailed Fist Song Book

'C' Battery moved to Teboursouk on 12 December and joined RHQ. The remainder of the Regiment was scattered over a wide area in individual troop and battery positions. At the end of the day 'C' Battery moved on to Testour and joined up with the 16th/5th Lancers who were acting as a reserve for 6th Armoured Division.

General Anderson now hoped that, although Allied units had withdrawn to Medjez-el-Bab, they could soon mount another offensive. New units were arriving from Algiers and plans were made for 78th Division to advance up the Medjerda Valley to take Tebourba and Djedeida and for 6th Armoured Division to move on their right flank to Massicault, before both divisions drove straight to Tunis.

As part of the reorganization required before this attack, 'C' Battery moved to Sloughia on 16 December and 'X' Troop was sent off to support 6th Battalion Royal Inniskilling Fusiliers in the hills south of Medjez. 16 December was also the day that the Battery received its first mail from home and after nightfall, it was observed by Captain Lincoln in a letter home, 'there was a lot of twinkling torches for some time afterwards'.

Letters from home were, of course, keenly anticipated. It took weeks, sometimes months, for letters and parcels to reach the troops in Tunisia. A long sea voyage and the possibility of ships being sunk by enemy action all contributed to late delivery, or no delivery at all. It was particularly galling to find in the pockets of German prisoners of war letters which had been posted in Germany only five days before. The importance of receiving news from home was vital for each individual's morale and happiness. The soldiers never could get enough letters; Mike Austin-Smith wrote a postscript in the form of a small advertisement in a letter to his parents, dated 27 January 1943: 'WANTED. Lonely soldier in N Africa wants plenty of mail.'

The next few days were uneventful and certainly not enlivened by the weather, which got increasingly worse with heavy rain and sleet. On 22 December, while carrying out a reconnaissance, the Commanding Officer, Lt Colonel Mansell, was wounded when his scout car drove over a mine. His Second in Command, Major J.A.T. Barstow, took over the command of the Regiment. 'Johnny B', as the new CO was known, had joined 'B' Battery HAC in 1929 and had embraced the chance of soldiering in the HAC with dedication and enthusiasm. He was a solicitor by profession and even in uniform still looked the part. Avuncular and amiable, he took a keen interest in everyone and developed a very special regimental spirit in which everyone was part of his much loved HAC family. But for all his humanity he did not lack offensive spirit. Almost the first thing that Lt Colonel Barstow did was to issue his first operations order, the last paragraph of which read:

FINALLY
The Regiment is about to engage in a period of hard and difficult fighting. We have a high tradition of fighting to maintain and our officers and men are of first rate qual-

ity and have been well trained. Remember that victory will go to the side that can keep fighting for 5 minutes longer than the enemy and that the success of this battle will depend on the personal determination and endurance of each one of us.

All great and honourable actions are accompanied with great difficulties and must be enterprised and overcome with answerable courage.

22 December 1942
J.A.T. Barstow[1]

But the time for honourable action did not come immediately; the offensive was postponed the next day because of torrential rain. Christmas Day was just as wet and miserable. 'X' Troop was in action and was visited by Major Rae, who recalled how the men tried to make the best of things:

> I shall always remember on that Christmas morning seeing a sub-section of 'X' Troop in action, making preparations for the Christmas dinner. A few compo boxes with a blanket made the table, the 'V' matches of the compo providing the only colour, and the issue chocolate, broken up into small squares, pooled in a glass bowl in the centre of the table. Compared with the surrounding mud this proved an attractive sight. Cover was provided by a tarpaulin.[2]

Compo rations were one of the great surprises of the campaign. They came in 14-man packs and were labelled with different letters of the alphabet, each one signifying different contents. Box A was very popular, containing steak and kidney, treacle pudding, chocolate and cigarettes. They were a real treat after austere Blighty rations. During the bad weather rum was issued as well.

Thankfully, the weather cleared two days later and 'C' Battery found itself supporting the 2nd Coldstream, who had tried so valiantly, and ultimately in vain, to capture Longstop Hill five miles north of Medjez.

When New Year's Eve finally arrived, the Battery was out of action so everyone was able to celebrate. Officers and Sergeants had a ration of a bottle of whisky or gin a month – happily, the ration had turned up in time. Other ranks were able to get hold of some rough local red wine, which they collected in jerry cans; the taste of petrol, no doubt, gave it a little extra *Je ne sais quoi!*

The New Year started with the Battery supporting two tank sweeps south-east of Medjez. The object was to locate the enemy's positions. The operation, entitled Bubble and Squeak, was a flop. They failed to find the enemy and a number of OP tanks got bogged down, including the Crusader tanks of Major Rae and Captain Lincoln.

The problem facing the Army Commander was that he had too few men to attack Tunis and, due to the increasing strength of the Germans, he was going to be hard pressed to defend the ground he had already won. He therefore declared his intention:

To contain the enemy by constant pressure and by limited attacks, to seize ground required to facilitate a later offensive, plans for which were to be prepared. All attacks to have maximum artillery support. To be ready to advance, even without armour, if the enemy moved troops away southwards.[3]

General Anderson knew that, ultimately, time was on his side because not only was he receiving more reinforcements but also General Montgomery's 8th Army, having won the Battle of El Alamein, was pursuing Rommel's Afrika Korps across the sands of Libya towards Tunisia. In the meantime, the initiative lay with the German troops in Tunisia, now called the 5th Panzer Army, under the command of the experienced Colonelgeneral Jürgen von Arnim.

General von Arnim's first step was to obtain some *Lebensraum* for his troops. Accordingly, he planned an operation called *Eilbote* (Express Messenger), with the object of attacking and occupying the main passes along the Eastern Dorsal, starting at Bou Arada in the north and including Kairouan, Fondouk and Faid further south.

As a preliminary move to their offensive, the Germans had captured a small hill with two trees on the top of it, which lay about five miles north-east of Bou Arada. Two Tree Hill, as it became known, was tactically important, because it was higher than its neighbours. Elements of 10th Rifle Brigade and 17th/21st Lancers, supported by 'D' and 'F' Batteries of 12th Regiment, tried in vain to recapture Two Tree Hill between 10 and 12 January 1943. On the dark and miserable night of 12 January, 'C' Battery moved south to join up with the rest of the Regiment so as to be ready to support another attack on Two Tree Hill the next morning.

The plan of attack was that the 6th Inniskilling (the Skins) were to advance, with OP officers on foot or in a carrier. As far as 'C' Battery was concerned, Lt Edwards went on foot and Captain Hunt rode in a carrier. Major Rae and Captain Lincoln were just able to set up an OP with the help of an officer from another Battery, who knew the ground. As dawn broke the telephone line had just been laid to the OP and the Battery started registering targets. The attack was not a success: the Skins found themselves pinned down by machine-guns, which were so well installed in the rocky hillside that not even shell fire could harm them. Finally, the Skins fell back under cover of a smoke screen put down by the Regiment. They had been given too tough a nut to crack and had suffered 100 casualties in their attempt. The experiment of sending FOOs with the infantry was not repeated because the officers could not see properly and their telephone lines were repeatedly being cut either by enemy fire or by the tracks of infantry carriers.

The next four days saw more 6th Armoured Division artillery reinforcing 12th Regiment and plans were made for a two-battalion attack on the obstinate Two Tree Hill. However, unbeknown to them, Operation *Eilbote* was ready to start on the same day.

12th Regiment was deployed on either side of the road from Goubellat to Bou Arada (see map, page 49). 'D' Battery was nearest to the enemy – on the east side

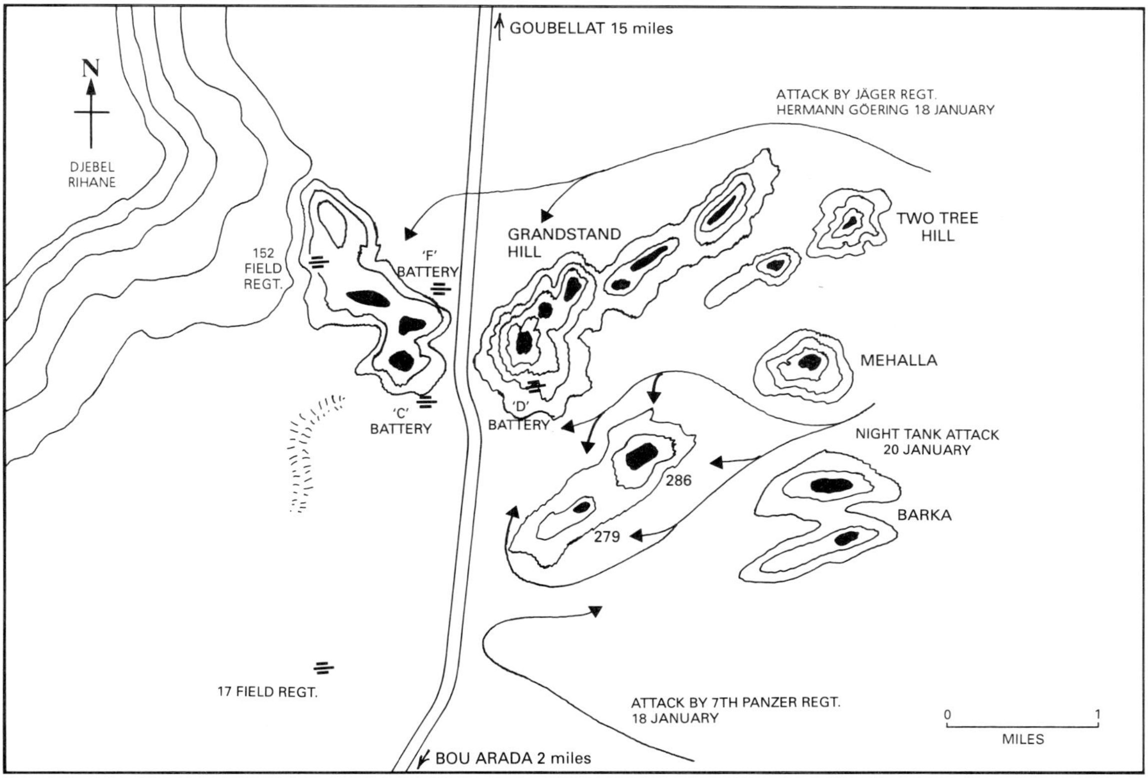

N
GOUBELLAT 15 miles
ATTACK BY JÄGER REGT.
HERMANN GÖERING 18 JANUARY
DJEBEL
RIHANE
GRANDSTAND
HILL
TWO TREE
HILL
152
FIELD
REGT.
'F'
BATTERY
MEHALLA
'C'
BATTERY
'D'
BATTERY
NIGHT TANK ATTACK
20 JANUARY
286
BARKA
279
17 FIELD REGT.
ATTACK BY 7TH PANZER REGT.
18 JANUARY
0
1
MILES
BOU ARADA 2 miles

In the above map, the 38th Irish Infantry Brigade held positions on Grandstand and the high ground to the west adjacent to 'F' Battery and 152 Field Regiment.

of the road tucked into a feature known as Grandstand Hill. 'C' and 'F' Batteries were placed at each end of a hill, on which there were some old Roman ruins, on the west side of the road. The German attack started with an attempt by 1st and 3rd Battalions of the Jäger Regiment Hermann Goering to outflank Grandstand Hill and to get among the Irish Brigade. This attack was resolutely resisted by the Faughs* and the Skins, supported by the 152nd (Ayrshire Yeomanry) Field Regiment RA. As the morning mist began to lift more German infantry could be seen advancing towards Grandstand Hill, where Colonel Barstow had installed himself in an OP with 'D' Battery, well positioned to direct the supporting artillery.

> When the battle was at its height Lieutenant-Colonel Barstow saw in the plain below him a fresh enemy battle group, including 30 tanks making as if to turn the Division's right flank at Bou Arada, so that it was now about to be attacked from a third side. He immediately engaged them with his other two batteries, 'D' at this moment being engaged at close range and fighting for its life.

*The nickname for the Royal Irish Fusiliers.

Major Stanley Rae took over 'C' Battery after Major Grose was wounded. He continued to command the Battery until September 1944.

His adjutant called the CRA to ask for the use of the whole divisional artillery and at the same time rounding up the other regiments on the net; the scene of ordered confusion in his command post must be imagined: fire orders and information of the battle arriving, the screeching of the radio operators into their microphones, the adjutant apparently speaking on the telephone and the radio, and giving verbal orders to his assistants all at once. He was soon able to report to his commanding officer that he was 'through' to one more regiment and one of the medium batteries, which were immediately ordered to engage. Colonel Barstow was therefore the first officer to engage an 'Uncle Target' using the new procedures in war in the history of the Royal Artillery. He found it easy and simple to operate, there was no need for any drastic corrections and the concentrations were very tight: no mere sprinkling of shells but a clump of bursts, the smoke all merging into one, so pleasing to a field gunner's eye. The thrust in the plain was stopped.[4]

This was a most successful day's work, with the guns firing 300 rounds each and causing the enemy heavy casualties and the loss of eight tanks. The day was marred for 'C' Battery, though, by the death of BSM R. Mackenzie. He was sitting with his back to a stone in the Roman ruin which served as 'X' Troop's Command Post, eating his lunch from a mess tin. One shell fell just in front of him. He got up with his mess tin in his hand, took two steps forward and fell down dead. Sergeant-Major Mackenzie was buried that night as the darkness in front of 'C' Battery's position was lit by the thudding explosions of British Sappers blowing up the hulks of the knocked-out German tanks. Sergeant J. Derricott took his place as TSM.

The next day everyone's attention was drawn to two low hills which lay to the south of Grandstand and were shown as Points 279 and 286 on the map. Both hills were occupied by the enemy. A reconnaissance by a company of the Skins, supported by divisional artillery, successfully reached Pt 286 but retired later according to plan. On 20 January 2nd London Irish Rifles were ordered to attack and occupy both Points 279 and 286. Captain Hunt went forward as an FOO in a carrier with his OP ACK Gunner R.H. Newell, an 18 set and a line-laying party of four men with two miles of wire. Captain Hunt was under the command of Major Hamilton Campbell of 'B' Battery 152nd Ayrshire Yeomanry. They set off before first light and, together with a company of the LIR, occupied Point 279 without any problems, except that the telephone line was fouled and could not reach the gun position.

German Mark IV tank knocked out during the Battle of Bou Arada on 18 January 1943. It was subsequently blown up by the Sappers on the same night. Note the corpse of one of the tank crew in the foreground.

Although they could hear plenty of small arms fire, there seemed to be no actual fighting and since they had seen the enemy retiring from Point 286, they suspected that the hill was no longer occupied. This fact was confirmed by a German medical orderly whom they captured when he came forward to help two wounded machine-gunners. Captain Hunt reported the good news to Major Hamilton Campbell, who was not far away, and proceeded to advance on to Point 286 itself, taking on targets when he could. Here he was joined by the Major. It was altogether an astonishing episode for 'C' Battery's OP party to capture the objective by themselves. Such is the fog of war! Later they returned in good order and the LIR sent forward a company to take over this troublesome hill.

Back in the gun areas there had been trouble for 'C' Battery in the form of a

51

Grave of BSM
*R. Mackenzie, who
was killed during the
Battle of Bou Arada on
18 January 1943. He
was buried on the Bat-
tery's position.*

heavy dive-bombing attack by Stukas. As usual men reached for their personal weapons to fire at the planes. This was standard practice, as one of them commented: 'You did feel better firing at the bastards and it did help to keep them coming low.'[5]

But this time the Stukas were pressing home their attacks. Gunner D. Cooper and L/Bombardier A. Williams were killed outright, and Gunner S. Rimmer died later from his wounds. Six others were wounded: Sergeant S. Newell, L/Bombardier V.S. Woodage and Gunners G.N. Barnes, C.L. Ramsey, F. Pollen and F. Stephenson. Donald Cooper was a particular loss to the Battery. He had gained the respect of his comrades by his deeply felt religious convictions. He had often organized small prayer meetings and there is little doubt that he would have become a priest after the war, had he lived.

It was not the nature of the German army to give up ground easily and indeed it was a standard drill that if one of its positions were captured, it would counter-attack quickly. So it was on the night of 20 January:

> The German counter-attack came in like a visitation from the angels of hell, complete with chariots of fire. The force and vigour of the onslaught was only matched by its audacity. True disciples of Rommel, the tank Commanders rode in, sitting in the turret tops armed with Very pistols and star shells to guide them. They simply charged along the ridge from one end to the other with a solid phalanx of tanks, leaving their Jägers to pick up the bits later ... Our defence dissolved into fragments before them.[6]

If the Panzers had driven straight on they would have engulfed 'C' Battery's

BSM J.E. Derricott took over from BSM Mackenzie as TSM 'X' Troop.

position. As it was, they went through 'D' Battery's old position, which had fortunately been vacated (they had been ordered south the night before). But the 7th Panzer Regiment had done everything and more than they had hoped for and had then retired. The LIR, who had been pitch-forked into this battle from the beginning, had suffered grievously, with the loss of 248 men. Also lost that night was Lt A.P. Davies of 'F' Battery, who was acting as an FOO for the Regiment and was captured by the enemy.

The wretched hill they had fought so hard for was solid rock and afterwards it was tacitly agreed by both sides as being virtually indefensible, although it might have helped the Irish Riflemen if they had actually armed the anti-tank mines they had laid in front of their position.[7]

After this attack the fighting around Two Tree Hill died down and 'C' Battery stayed there under the command of 152nd Regiment Ayrshire Yeomanry. Operation *Eilbote* was still under way and, although 10th Panzer Division had been beaten off at Bou Arada, the enemy 334th Mountain Division made a successful attack on the French further south. Woefully ill-equipped, the French were forced to retire with the loss of a considerable number of men and badly needed equipment. British and American units were rushed to shore up this part of the front and successfully held off the German threat. Some of these units were energetically supported by 'D' and 'F' Batteries. During 'C' Battery's stay at Bou Arada, it was delighted to find itself supporting a new unit, 3rd Grenadier Guards. This was the beginning of a happy relationship which lasted throughout the campaign.

'C' Battery was next called south and on 6 February found itself supporting a French battalion in the Region of Robaa. It also supported the notorious Moroccan mounted infantry, Les Goumières, known as the Goums. These bloodthirsty fighters, who wore striped cloaks and turbans, had a penchant for cutting off their enemy's ears as souvenirs. Lt Ian Miller, the Battery's 'French expert', went on a mounted patrol with some of them, accompanied by his signallers. Alas, although they were RHA, one of them thought that when his horse bolted he was going to be the first Allied soldier to arrive in Tunis!

By and large though, the Battery had a fairly quiet time until 16 February, when the whole Regiment was ordered to Maktar about 70 miles to the south-west. There was a feeling of tension in the air and rumours of heavy German attacks in the south. No sooner had 'C' Battery harboured at Maktar in the early hours of 17 February, than it was ordered to move again to Sbiba as quickly as possible. The Battery Commander went on ahead and when he arrived he was fascinated to find a 1st Army staff officer talking on the civilian line to the Army Commander, General Anderson. Shortly afterwards General Keightley, the GOC 6th Armoured Division, arrived along with Brigadier V. Copeland-Griffiths, Commander of 1st Guards Brigade. Something serious was obviously up, but what?

The Germans had achieved most of their objectives in Operation *Eilbote* by taking the passes at Kairouan, Fondouk and Faid. But General von Arnim was aware that time was not on their side. Montgomery's 8th Army had already reached Tripoli and was pressing on towards the Mareth Line in southern Tunisia. Furthermore, Axis forces in Africa were receiving less than half the supplies they needed because their communications with Sicily and Italy were struggling under the increasing stranglehold of the Allied navies and air forces.

A plan was devised whereby von Arnim would attack the Americans at Maknassy and Sidi Bou Zid, before driving on to Sbeitla and Kasserine, where he hoped to join up with Rommel's Afrika Assault Korps, who were going to advance via Gafsa to Feriana and Kasserine. These two operations were code-named *Frühlingswind* (Spring Breeze) and *Morgensluft* (Morning Airs). It was hoped that by the time they joined up at Kasserine these 'light breezes' would have increased to gale force and, once through the Kasserine Pass, they would blow their way north as far as Bone on the coast, thereby destroying the American forces and isolating the British and French from Algiers. It was a bold plan which nearly worked.

When 'C' Battery arrived at Sbiba on 17 February they were told to support 3rd Grenadier Guards while 'D' Battery supported 2nd Coldstream in a position about 10 miles south of Sbiba, guarding a pass which led to Le Kef in the north. As 'C' Battery took up its position it found a large number of Americans moving to the rear. These inexperienced, poorly trained and now very tired troops told anyone who cared to listen that Rommel was right behind them. This did not worry anyone. 'After all,' recollected L/Bombardier Allan Lewis, 'this was "C" Battery with the "Grenadiers" and the "Coldstreams" in front of us!' His confidence was subsequently justified.

The Germans finally attacked on 19 February with 30–40 tanks and infantry. The morning mist lifted to reveal the enemy column, which was immediately en-

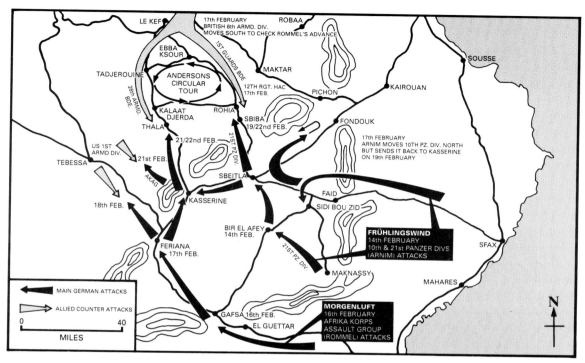

The German attack on Kasserine lasted from 14 to 23 February. 10th Panzer Division had their own circular tour, having been ordered to Fondouk and then told to turn round and join Rommel at Kasserine. Perhaps they had their own version of 'It's all been changed'; for example, 'Vorwärts Marsch! Alle Mann zurück! Es ist jetzt alles anders!'

gaged to good effect by both 'C' and 'D' Batteries. But later, 'D' Battery found its position under threat by German tanks halted on a ridge about 400 yards away. During the afternoon these tanks withdrew one by one on being engaged by a single gun of 'C' Battery.

The following day, the 21st Panzer Division attacked again, and again were beaten off by 'C' Battery firing 150 rounds per gun. Daybreak on 21 February revealed some German troops dug in about 1000 yards away from Captain Lincoln's OP, which was on high ground, and he was therefore able to make their lives a misery. It was, he recalled, 'dream shooting'. In the afternoon the OP was able to witness a remarkable action made by some Churchill tanks (the first to be used in Tunisia) manned by the North Irish Horse. The Churchills made a reconnaissance on a hill at the same time as some German tanks approached the same hill from the opposite direction. The OP could not communicate with the North Irish Horse and it was a race to get to the top. It turned out to be a dead heat and a sharp battle broke out on the summit. In the end both sides withdrew, each having had three tanks knocked out.

On the evening of 22 February, 'C' and 'D' Batteries withdrew to Rohia, about 10 miles to the north of Sbiba, where a shorter line could be held. There was no contact with the enemy on 23 February because they had withdrawn, and 'C' and 'D' Batteries were ordered to move by a circular route to join up with 'F' Battery, who had been doing great things at Thala on the road between Kasserine and Le Kef. There was a shorter route across the hills but no one knew where the enemy were and it was considered too risky. The night was cold, wet and very dark. The column finally arrived at Kalaat Djerda, a few miles short of Thala, at 0600 hours the next day. They had no sooner arrived than they received orders to return to Rohia, whence they had come. This time they chanced the short route and arrived at about noon. They had scarcely had time to get anything to eat when that dreaded order came: 'Prepare to move!' Believe it or not, they were ordered to Thala again. 'Haven't you heard, it's all been changed!' The regimental column finally arrived at Thala at 1900 hours in total darkness, having been on the move for 24 hours in the most miserable conditions. This highly frustrating and exhausting drive became known as 'Anderson's Circular Tour'. The confusion was probably caused by doubt at 1st Army HQ about which of the two roads to Le Kef was the most vulnerable to the enemy.

By 24 February the road from Sbiba to Le Kef had been made safe but the 10th Panzer Division, under the personal command of Rommel, had forced the Kasserine Pass on 20 February and had driven back a small US force under Colonel Stack. Tanks of the British 26th Armoured Brigade came to their aid on the same day but were forced to fight a bitter rearguard action. As darkness fell the German tanks overran a battalion of the Leicesters and infiltrated 'F' Battery's position. Realizing that they had unwelcome guests in their midst, 'F' Battery knocked out three German tanks with three shots. All next day 'F' Battery formed part of the front line 'with nothing in front!' and earned honour for themselves and the Regiment. By the time 'C' and 'D' Batteries arrived, although they did not know it at the time, Rommel had shot his bolt and his forces had withdrawn.

The road through the pass though was heavily mined and in the follow-up operation several vehicles were blown up, including Captain Hunt's 8cwt. He was severely shaken and his driver Maurice Harvey had a cut lip and a badly bruised foot, but nothing worse (as was standard, the floor of the vehicle was sandbagged against mines).

On 26 February the Regiment withdrew from the line and had a good night's sleep. It certainly deserved it. The men now looked forward to a proper rest and a refit but almost immediately these hopes were dashed and they found themselves retracing their steps over the 120 miles to El Aroussa, 10 miles west of Bou Arada. General von Arnim, believing 1st Army to be off balance because of their need to rush forces to Kasserine, had therefore launched a series of attacks in the northern sector, code-named *Ochsenkopf* (Oxhead). It was one of these attacks that the Guards Brigade and 12th Regiment were required to resist. At this time the Guards started calling themselves the 'Plumbers' because they were always plugging holes in the line, and 12th Regiment, who were supporting them, were proud to be known as the 'Plumbers' Mates'.

On 28 February a company of 2nd Coldstream, supported by some Churchill tanks of 51st RTR and the guns of 12th Regiment, attacked Steam Roller Farm on the northern slopes of Djebel Rihane. Although the Coldstreams were pinned down by enemy fire and several Churchills were knocked out, one Churchill managed to get into the farm and caused absolute carnage. The next day 3rd Grenadiers renewed the attack, to find that the enemy had fled leaving a number of vehicles and a considerable amount of supplies, which were quickly looted by all and sundry. Among other things, two BMW motorcycle combinations were acquired and issued to 'X' and 'W' Troops.

The weather was still bad but, from time to time, it was possible to get a bath in the natural hot-sulphur baths at Beja. A number of officers and men were able to get away for 48 hours' leave in a French holiday hotel at Ain Draham. Finally, the Regiment was pulled back to Sakiet Sidid Youssef on the Algerian border to concentrate with 6th Armoured Division. The armoured units were issued with Sherman tanks whose 75mm guns ensured that at last they had a tank which could compete with the Germans and was able to destroy enemy anti-tank guns at long range.

While 6th Armoured Division trained with its new equipment, Montgomery's 8th Army was attacking the Afrika Korps on the Mareth Line. It finally outflanked this heavily defended position on 27 March and started to advance deeper into Tunisia, pushing the enemy steadily northwards. A determined attempt was needed to try to intercept the Afrika Korps before it joined up with von Arnim's army in the north. This attempt was entrusted to Lt General John Crocker's 9th Corps, which included 6th Armoured Division, elements of 46th Infantry Division and the US 34th (Red Bull) Division.

6th Armoured Division first moved to Sbiba in order to mislead the enemy and on 5 April the whole Division made a night march of about 30 miles northwards to El Ala, 11 miles west of the Fondouk Pass. It was hoped that it would be possible to storm the Pass and then to drive straight for Kairouan and the sea, thereby cutting off the Afrika Korps as it retreated north.

12th Regiment was part of 26th Armoured Brigade, now commanded by one of the most skilful commanders of British armour in the war, Brigadier 'Pip' Roberts. At last the Regiment would be able to play the role for which it had been trained, namely to support armour. The plan was that the heights to the north and south of the Fondouk Pass would be attacked by 3rd Welsh Guards and men of the US 34th Division respectively. When the high ground had been secured, 26th Armoured Brigade would advance through the Pass and onwards to the sea.

General Sir Harold Alexander gave orders that the Pass must be taken come what may, otherwise the Afrika Korps would escape. The Corps Commander, Lt General John Crocker, passed on these orders directly to Brigadier Roberts. Colonel Barstow, who was present, recalled that 'It was a clear example of the personality and determination of a commander influencing the battle by being in the right place at the right time. I was thrilled to be there.' But Brigadier Roberts and

'Plumbers' – 3rd Battalion Grenadier Guards looking particularly non-plussed, no doubt at the prospect of descending a steep wadi to do another plumbing job! Kasserine Pass, February 1943.

the 17th/21st Lancers were certainly not thrilled to be there. They thought the Pass must be mined and covered by enemy anti-tank guns. They were quite right.

Major Charles Nix, whose squadron was to lead the advance, remembered his regimental history when the 17th Lancers charged into 'the Valley of Death' at Balaclava in the charge of the Light Brigade. 'Goodbye,' he said, turning to a brother officer. 'We shall all be killed.' 12th Regiment put down smoke to cover 17th/21st Lancers' advance and fired HE at the German positions in the Pass. The 17th/21st Lancers advanced and were blown up on mines and shot up by anti-tank guns as they feared. Major Nix was killed, but not before he and his men had seriously damaged the enemy's defences. It was a stalemate though. But then some tanks on the left thought there might be a way round by using a dry river bed. 16th/5th Lancers were ordered to explore this possibility, and succeeded. Captain Lincoln, who was with them as FOO, had been sitting in his tank feeling very bored up to then, so much so that he had started to read a copy of *The Tatler* which he had received in the mail the day before. Much to his delight he saw a picture of his father. After that his headset began crackling and he was ordered to advance and indeed was the first gunner through the Pass. In the meantime the Welsh Guards had taken their objective but the Americans succeeded only the next day, when the opposition had withdrawn under cover of darkness.

The next morning the whole of 6th Armoured Division poured through the Fondouk Pass along paths laid through the minefields by the Sappers during the night. Once they were through, the Division created a box formation and advanced in full cry over the plain. This mass of tanks and vehicles ploughing through the wheat, bespeckled with yellow daisies and red poppies, was an exhilarating sight. Everyone was in high spirits. The war correspondent Alan Moorehead wrote:

'Mates' – a 25-pounder in action somewhere in Tunisia, 1 March 1943. Note the gun has just fired and the barrel is at maximum recoil with the No.2 just about to eject the cartridge. Regiment unknown.

I found myself in the midst of the most exultant and exciting spectacle as a war can offer – a victorious army rushing forward over its battlefields in pursuit of the enemy ... A strange buoyant excitement seized the army then. Men in their eagerness to rush on, do reckless things like running blindly through minefields. They feel they can't be stopped now, that every gun has twice the power it had before, that every man is equal to a dozen of the enemy. 'Get on ... get on...' You hear the order everywhere, and in the dust and the shouting and the confusion the men are laughing and talking at the top of their voices.[8]

This glorious pursuit met only a little opposition and the Battery was able to advance about 15 miles to a point near Kairouan. The next day, 11 April, the advance wheeled to the left towards Sbikha and everyone realized that the enemy had escaped: the attempt to cut them off had failed by 24 hours. This was not the only thing that rankled: professional pride had been injured because the OPs and the guns had been unable to keep up with the 16th/5th Lancers. The ground was covered with ditches and wadis, which tanks could easily overcome but wheeled vehicles could not. By this time 'C' Battery had only one 8cwt truck left for its OP party.

On 12 April 26th Armoured Brigade reached Sbikha and the Afrika Korps' rearguard. That same day they met forward units of the 8th Army; both armies regarded each other with a mixture of curiosity and weariness. But there was one unit of 8th Army that 12th Regiment was delighted to see and that was their former parent 11th HAC Regiment RHA. It was not long before the two Regiments found themselves side-by-side on the Goubellat–Bou Arada road north of their old battlegrounds near Two Tree Hill, which was still in enemy hands. Now the two armies were joined up (they were called 18th Army Group), General Alexander had a great superiority in men and materials over the enemy.

The plan to attack Tunis involved 5th Corps forcing its way from Medjez down the Medjerda Valley, something they could do only if they took the mountain peaks on each side of the river, including the dreaded Longstop. 6th Armoured Division with 1st Armoured Division (ex 8th Army) were, as part of 9th Corps, to advance eastwards over the Goubellat Plain in the hope that they would be able to take the two-peaked Djebel Bou Kournine (known as Twin Tits) and mislead the enemy about where the main attack was coming from. The whole operation was code-named Vulcan. But before Vulcan started the Hermann Goering Division made a spoiling attack, code-named, most improbably, Lilac Blossom. This attack was made all along the line of the road from Medjez to Bou Arada.

The regimental area was attacked in the early morning of 21 April by infantry and artillery. Nearly all that day the Regiment had to lie low and absorb the enemy fire because it was under orders not to retaliate and thereby disclose its position. Bombardier Peter McGregor and Gunner George Gould were killed by enemy shell fire. At the end of the day Brigadier Lyon-Smith became so exasperated with this one-way traffic that he gave the order for 10 rounds of gun fire to be fired at the German battery which could be clearly seen. Seldom were 10 rounds of gun fire fired with more enthusiasm. The results were highly satisfactory and the Regiment's tormentors suffered heavy casualties.

Thus was the Lilac Blossom blown away, at least as far as 6th Armoured Division were concerned. (It was also blown away by other units equally successfully further north.)

Operation Vulcan was not delayed, and started at 0200 hours on 22 April, with the Regiment shooting in the area of Two Tree Hill in support of 6th Yorks and Lancs. The guns fired 400 rounds each that day and satisfactory progress was made, although Two Tree Hill was evacuated by the enemy only that night. After that, 'C' Battery supported 16th/5th Lancers and advanced to the east side of what was known as the Sugar Lake (Sabkrat el Kourzia) under the lee of the menacing Djebel Kournine and many prisoners were taken. But 24 April proved to be a miserable day, for the Regiment had to endure heavy artillery and mortar fire directed by the German OPs on Kournine. Among the casualties were the Battery Commanders of 'D' and 'F' Batteries, Major Causton and Major Middleton.

Indeed, there was an overall shortage of officers, and BSMs and NCOs showed considerable leadership, courage and skill in serving the guns and command posts. Djebel Kournine presented too difficult a task at that moment and it was decided to withdraw, having successfully enticed the enemy's armour to concentrate in the rear of the mountain, away from the main attack in the north.

6th Armoured Division returned to where it had started, just south of Goubellat. In the reorganization caused by the officer casualties Captain Lincoln was promoted to command 'D' Battery. This was a natural reward for the unstinting and

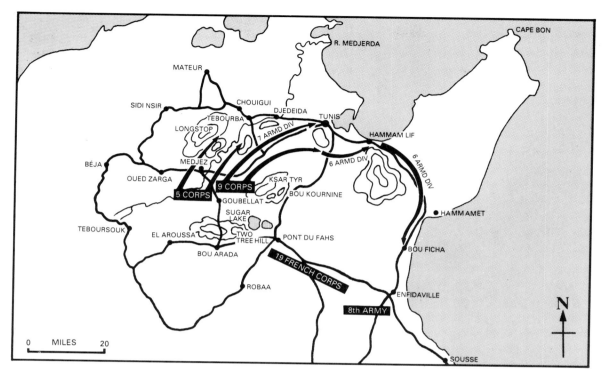

The final offensive on Tunis 6–13 May 1943. Tunis was captured on 7 May. Hammam Lif fell on 9 May and the enemy finally capitulated on 13 May.

skilful way in which he had performed his duties as leader of 'W' Troop and comparatively recently as Battery Captain.

The time had now come for the the final drive to Tunis. Essentially, the plan was very much the same as the plan that was aborted at Christmas because of the bad weather. The idea was that the infantry of 5th Corps were to advance down the Medjerda Valley, after they had taken the mountain defences on both sides of the Valley. The infantry divisions of 9th Corps would advance on a narrow front towards Massicault on the right flank of 5th Corps, allowing 6th and 7th Armoured Divisions to pass through them to maintain the momentum of the attack and then swing right to Tunis.

On 28 April, while preparing for the next attack, the Regiment held a church parade, which was bombed by Mitchells of the US Air Force; fortunately there were no casualties.

On 6 May the final advance began. 12th Regiment was on the right flank of 6th Armoured Division, supporting 201st Guards Brigade, ready if necessary to repulse any attack from the enemy in the region to the rear of a hill named Ksar Tyr. This threat did not materialize, although the advance was none too pleasant, as Colonel Barstow recollected:

The day was hot and sunny ... The improvised tracks had become inches, almost feet, deep in dust and we had to use a handkerchief as a filter through which to breathe. It was impossible to see a vehicle five yards in front ... The fine sunny day had been transformed into a November mist in London, from the smoke of shell fire, dust and burning vehicles.[9]

The next day that great Reconnaissance Regiment, the Derbyshire Yeomanry, entered Tunis. 6th Armoured Division was ordered to bypass the city and to attack the enemy at Hammam Lif. This was a particularly strong position; the mountains overlooking the town came down to within half a mile of the sea. The town was heavily defended by a mass of anti-tank guns and houses which had been turned into small fortresses. The Welsh Guards stormed the heights with great gallantry, Captain Hunt going forward to support their leading company.

By the next morning, 9 May, the high ground had been taken with the help of the Coldstreams but the town below was still holding out. Brigadier Lyon-Smith laid on an 'Uncle Target' – 40 rounds of gun fire which smashed into the town. The armoured regiments of 26th Armoured Brigade then advanced and the Lothian and Border Horse attacked with great dash, managing to outflank the town along the beach. By 10 May Hammam Lif had fallen in what had been a most remarkable feat of arms.

Orders were received for 201st Guards Brigade and 17th/21st Lancers, supported by 12th Regiment, to advance as quickly as possible during the night to Hammamet, thereby cutting off the Cape Bon peninsula. Everything was in frantic haste now and already large numbers of Italians and Germans were surrendering with hundreds of their vehicles.

By 13 May the Regiment found itself deployed in a position between Bou Ficha and Enfidaville, where the remnants of the Afrika Korps, the 90th Light Division, were still holding up the 8th Army. Now taken in the rear, the enemy was subjected to three waves of US bombers, each of 18 aircraft. The Regiment opened fire and as the British tanks went forward the OPs saw white flags appearing on the hillside. If no white flag was seen in an area, Captain 'Bob' Atherton, who was leading 'W' Troop, started ranging – immediately another white flag appeared.

An armoured car of the Derbyshire Yeomanry happened to be on 'W' Troop's position when it received a wireless message from the HQ of 1st Italian Army stating, in English, that they wanted to surrender 'with the honours of war'. After consultation with 6th Armoured Division, the Italians were told that they must surrender unconditionally. The Italians, who had been using perfect British signals procedure, replied 'Wait, over!' and then a little later agreed to surrender unconditionally. Six months to the day after 'C' Battery had landed in Algiers the fighting was over, the battle won.

CHAPTER SIX

Distant drums

Here with a Loaf of Bread beneath the Bough
A Flask of Wine, a book of Verse – and Thou
Beside me singing in the Wilderness –
And Wilderness is Paradise now.

'How sweet is mortal sovereignty!' – think some:
Others – 'How blest the Paradise to come!'
Ah, take the Cash in hand and waive the Rest:
Oh, the brave Music of a distant Drum!

The Rubaiyat of Omar Khayyam
Edward Fitzgerald

fter the realization that the war in North Africa was over, the general feeling was a mixture of amazement and relief. 'C' Battery had, in fact, taken a very active part in one of the most comprehensive military victories in history. Over 238,000 personnel of the Axis forces surrendered, of whom 101,000 were German. Also, a vast amount of military material was captured.

During the campaign the Allies had suffered 75,000 casualties. The British 1st Army accounted for a third of these, with 4,094 killed, 12,566 wounded and 9,082 missing, totalling 25,742.[1] 12th Regiment lost 42 officers and men killed, 13 of whom were from 'C' Battery. It is not possible to record how many were wounded. Where names are known, they have been mentioned. Quite often though, men who had been hurt or who were suffering from shock were patched up at an aid post and rested for a day or so before they returned to duty. They had become both physically and mentally very tough.

There has been little opportunity during the description of the last six months' fighting to describe the daily round, the common task of Battery life. Brigadier Ken Hunt, who was Captain of 'X' Troop for most of that time, recalled in a letter to the author that:

Victory parade in Tunis on 20 May 1943. 12th HAC Regiment provided a marching contingent consisting of representatives from all batteries led by their CO, Lt Colonel Johnny Barstow DSO, who complained in a letter to Armoury House about the indignity of RHA Gunners having to march 'on their poor old plates of meat!' The bulled-up gun barrels on the right bear the names of Longstop and Medjez-el-Bab.

'The BQMS and his boys had a hell of a job.' BQMS W.F. Collen-Jones – a much-respected stalwart of the Battery.

In Africa, gunpits had to be dug quickly, against the expected air attacks and possible shelling. Slit trenches too, fast. Then it would rain and all would fill with water. There were no tents (bivvies came much later), so improvised shelters had to be made and camouflaged, built over holes for shelter. All flanks were open – it was a big open space, sand, scrub, rock, mud according to whether one was in a fertile plain or in the foothills or mountains. There were no infantry to guard or patrol, they were far too stretched. So all had to be on the alert for ambushes – the German parachutists were really aggressive and bold, and fast with it, here and gone. We were never out of action, someone always wanted the guns. We supported, it seemed, everyone, moving great distances by night to be there in place (Anderson's Circular Tours, The Plumbers etc.). So there was no rest.

The BQMS and his boys had a hell of a job. Moving on horrendous roads by night (by day distinctly unsafe); mapread and find; drive an indifferent WD vehicle up a poor track; deliver the goods and then find the way back to get more supplies, ammo and so on to do it all again. Except that the Bty was now 70 miles away somewhere else.

It needed stalwart BSMs and GPOs to keep the gun position happy and efficient, and dry and as warm as maybe, and always ready for yet another move or more firing. There was a great sense of being on one's own – even the Bty was often scattered, the Regt almost always. The Germans could appear from anywhere and

their aircraft always did. But there was never time to get bored, just enough to get comfortable before having to up sticks.

For the first three weeks after the Axis surrender, the Regiment was based outside Hammamet and 'C' Battery, like everybody else, swam and sunbathed naked along the lovely beaches nearby. Needless to say, the Army did not let them off as easily as that. On 20 May there was a Victory Parade in Tunis, at which Generals Eisenhower and Anderson took the salute. The Battery sent a number of men to march in the parade; the 12th Regiment contingent was led by Lt Colonel Barstow, bemoaning the fact that 'the RHA were reduced to bashing gravel on their poor old plates of meat!' It was, by all accounts, a very good parade and the standard of drill and turnout was excellent, although one member of 'C' Battery observed that the crowd cheered especially loudly anyone who wore a red hat, including, to his disgust, the Military Police! Five days later the CRA Brigadier Lyon-Smith held his own parade for the Divisional artillery. Hospitality was exchanged between units and one of the more enjoyable parties was for the combined 80 officers and 150 sergeants of 11th and 12th Regiments HAC at Nabeul.

This pleasant sojourn was not to last and the Regiment, together with 6th Armoured Division, was ordered to move to Robertville, near Phillipeville on the north coast of Tunisia. On 17 June, on the way to their new quarters, they

Sergeants' Mess, Robertville, 1943. (Back row) Sgt Marchant, Sgt Phillips, L/Sgt Ferrari, Sgt Ashpole, Sgt Davis, BQMS Collen-Jones, L/Sgt Hudspith, Sgt Westcombe, Sgt Murray. (Middle row) Sgt Summers, L/Sgt Hellis, L/Sgt Farmer, L/Sgt Barnes, Sgt O'Brien, Sgt Fletcher, BSM Pearston, BSM Derricott, Sgt Newell. (Front row) L/Sgt Hendey, Sgt Bryant, Sgt Knight, Sgt Harrison, L/Sgt McAndrew.

Regimental Theatre, Robertville, 1943. Amateur shows were put on at any convenient time throughout the war at both Battery and Regimental levels. The Regiment was also visited by ENSA parties. Note the mailed fist of 6th Armoured Division.

paused at Penthièvre, where the Divisional artillery was inspected by the Captain General of the HAC, King George VI.

The Regiment finally settled alongside a dusty road by the side of a hill covered with scrub and olive trees. This was certainly no paradise and it was not long before it was known as 'Death Valley'. To start with, there were only primitive tents and bivouacs. The temperature was 100°F or more in the shade and soon it became obvious that this was a most unhealthy place. Men started going sick with malaria, jaundice, desert sores and probably the worst illness of all, dysentery. Immense efforts were taken to combat the malarial mosquitoes. All troops were ordered to take the disgusting mepacrim tablets; green foliage was cut down and streams and ponds were sprayed with chemicals to try to wipe out the mosquito breeding grounds; long trousers and long-sleeved shirts were compulsory at dusk, and everyone slept under nets at night. However, despite all these efforts, the mosquito menace was not eliminated.

Men who were seriously ill were sent to either a British or Canadian field general hospital. In both they were well looked after but the Canadian hospital was considered better because the discipline was less formal, and the patients were known as the 'sick and amorous division'.

One of the problems for a patient was that when he recovered he was at risk of being posted to another unit. Both officers and men went to much trouble to see that they returned to 'C' Battery. So anxious was L/Sergeant Jack Farmer that he decided to discharge himself, and hitch-hiked back to 'C' Battery only to find a rather strange reception. This was because he had been posted as a

deserter! How anyone could imagine that such a stalwart of 'X' Troop's Command Post could have any thought in his head other than to do his duty for his Battery, his Regiment and his country, would be very hard to say. In fact, Jack Farmer had malaria again, and again he walked out to get back to 'C' Battery, to find that this time he had been posted only as AWOL.

It was one of the ironies of the military existence that the average soldier was far more likely to become a casualty because of an accident or illness than because of battle. This is illustrated below. The figures refer to 1000 ration strength per annum for the Middle East in 1943.[2]

battle casualties	22
non-battle casualties	49
sickness	442

'C' Battery officers' reunion, Robertville, 1943. (Left to right) Stratton Holland, Geoff Lowe, Dick Foulkes, Ken Hunt, Stanley Rae, Tom Lacey, Freddie Woodward, Aubrey Lincoln, Douglas Hughes, Philip Rooke, Bob Atherton, Richard Young, Jack Edwards, Mike Austin-Smith, Peter Ongley, Eric Freeman.

As time went by, camp facilities improved. Nissen huts were provided to act as canteens for each battery. Men were able to place their tents against the hillside, digging out the soil and turning their abodes into little parlours with inglenook fireplaces made out of petrol tins, and generally trying to make them as homely as possible. Games and sports were played regularly, including rugby, soccer and boxing. 'C' Battery had a number of good soccer players, such as Tom White, Jock Abbie, Bert Scott, Jack Marchant and Alf Titterton. The Church of Scotland contributed a canteen and there was an Engineers' hut in which concerts of classical music were played on gramophone records,

Lt Colonel J.A.T. Barstow DSO MC, CO *of 12th* HAC *Regiment* RHA. *Major General Keightley* CB DSO, GOC *6th Armoured Division. Brigadier T. Lyon-Smith* DSO, CRA *6th Armoured Division.*

usually in total darkness. A stage was built and not only did ENSA touring parties play there but also the Regiment put on its own shows, with Captain Mike Austin-Smith and Gunner Gordon Thomas, among others, showing off their thespian talents.

Officers and men were able to get away to either of the nearby towns – Phillipeville or Constantine. Sometimes it was possible to go to Algiers. But there were no proper facilities for other ranks to relax. Beer was in short supply but there were ample quantities of the rough red wine available in the cafés and bars. Although the notorious Casbah was out of bounds (which did not deter everyone!), there were brothels available, which no doubt did a 'whoring trade'! The 'Sphinx' and the 'Black Cat' were two quite large establishments. Officers had better facilities for leave and recreation; they also had more opportunity to meet 'nice' girls, either in French families or among the nurses from the hospitals. Here is a description of the end of a fancy dress party held at the Canadian hospital, supplied by Captain Austin-Smith in a letter of 4 November 1943:

> We finished up with some terrific singing, with the Matron, Colonel and Padre all joining in. The complete lack of any self-consciousness, the terrific energy and spirit they showed made the whole thing radiate with enjoyment. It really was one of the best parties I have ever been to, especially when you consider it was in a tent in the middle of a stubble field in the wilds of N.A.

In such convivial circumstances it was scarcely surprising that Gunner Cupid hit some targets with his amorous arrows!

During August 1943, all the 25-pounders were withdrawn and replaced by

G.E. Thomas. Mon 10 Jan 44

Priests. These were 105mm self-propelled guns based on the chassis of a Sherman tank and they could fire a 33lb shell a distance of 12,200 yards. They had a number of advantages over the 25-pounders. First, they protected the crew against small arms fire and shell splinters; moreover, they had a 0.5 Browning AA gun mounted on an armoured pulpit. Second, each gun was a mobile gun position, which meant that from the moment a fire order was issued by the OP, the target could be plotted on the artillery board, and the guns laid and the first ranging round fired within three minutes. Third, the Priest was highly mobile and could keep up with the armour despite the difficult going. Fourth, the gun used flashless powder, which meant that GPOs did not need to worry about extensive cover. The Priest's main defect was that it

At Robertville in the winter months of 1943–44, tents were made as comfortable as possible. Note pin-ups, bookshelf and boxed blankets.

had a low muzzle velocity and could not be used in the same way as the 25-pounder in an anti-tank role.

The equipment was American and this meant that a great deal of retraining was necessary. Sights were graduated in 'mils' instead of degrees, dial sights became 'panoramic telescopes', directors became 'aiming circles'. With the Priests came US vehicles such as the White Scout Car and half tracks, all of which were fitted out by the Battery artificers with stands for wireless sets, special tables and other furnishings. Sherman tanks were issued to the OPs. The 75mm gun was replaced by a wooden barrel, allowing room in the turret for three wireless sets. It was now possible to recharge the wireless batteries by using an auxiliary motor in the tank. This saved a lot of time and hard work which had previously been spent humping heavy batteries about.

In all, the Battery spent 10 months at Robertville. When the weather became cooler the mosquitoes disappeared and everyone was able to spend a reasonably warm and comfortable winter there. There were a number of changes in personnel. Captain Lincoln returned for a few weeks before departing to take command of 'B' Battery 152nd Regiment Ayrshire Yeomanry for the rest of the war, which he did with much distinction. Captain Philip Rooke joined the Battery as Battery Captain, and Captain Mike Austin-Smith was posted from 'F' Battery to become the leader of 'X' Troop. (Both Captains Rooke and Austin-Smith were exceptional in that they had been members of 'C' Battery before they went to OCTU and on being commissioned they not only returned to 12th Regiment but also served with 'C' Battery again.) At a higher level, Brigadier 'Tiger' Lyon-Smith left the Division to become the CRA for 7th Armoured Division, which had been sent back to England to train for the cross-Channel invasion. He had done much to create a very high standard of efficiency among the gunner regiments under his command.

> In action, his personal leadership and his personal direction of fire was at all times an inspiration to Regimental officers. His offensive spirit pervaded the whole Divisional Artillery and materially affected the fighting ability of these regiments.[3]

A story typical of the Brigadier's 'offensive spirit' refers to the time when he came upon a 'C' Battery gunner holding a Tommy gun. 'What are you intending to do with that weapon?' asked the redoubtable 'Tiger'. The gunner explained that it was to help him defend himself against the enemy. 'It is certainly not,' came the reply. 'It is for attacking Germans and killing them!'

But before Brigadier Lyon-Smith left in December 1943, he addressed the Battery and told them how the war was going and what their part was likely to be. By 17 August Sicily had been captured by the Allied forces. After this the British 8th Army invaded the toe of Italy and ultimately linked up with an Allied force that had landed south of Naples at Salerno. Mussolini had fallen and Italy had surrendered. Under one of their most skilful generals, Field Marshal Albert Kesselring,* the Germans had rushed forces south and had started a series of hard-fought defensive actions in a country tailor-made for defence.

During the first three months of 1944 the drums of war beat louder as the Battery prepared itself and its equipment to be shipped to Italy. Special attention was paid to training and getting to know the 16th/5th Lancers, whom they were going to support in the campaign to come. To date this campaign had not been going well. The Allied armies were stuck in front of the German Gustav Line, which was about 80 miles south of Rome and ran from coast to coast, bolstered by the daunting monastery at Cassino and the towering mountains behind it (see map, page 74). Three times in three months American, British, Canadian, French, Indian, New Zealander and Polish troops attacked Cassino and three times they were bloodily repulsed.

An attempt to outflank the Gustav Line by a landing at Anzio had been equally fruitless and was contained by an energetic and well-organized German defence. Most of the fighting had been taking place in the appalling conditions of an Italian winter. Robertville might not have been much fun but it was infinitely preferable to being in the front line at Anzio or Cassino.

6th Armoured Division was required to take part in the next onslaught and 12th Regiment embarked its vehicles and component parts at the ports of Algiers, Bizerta and Bone. 'C' Battery sailed from Bone on the SS *Askania* on 3 April 1944.

---

* Not only was Field Marshal Kesselring one of Hitler's most competent generals; he also possessed a quality probably rare among that company – he had a sense of humour. After the war he was escorted to a prison by a charming Jewish officer of the 4th Hussars who, as the air thawed in the back of the staff-car, was soon exchanging photographs with the old man: 'That is my wife, ach she is an ambitious woman. When I had been a Field Marshal for three years she told me: "Albert you will never get anywhere, you do not push yourself enough".'

Loopy, George Kennard, p. 78.

CHAPTER SEVEN

*Sempre avanti!**

Niente Mangario   *Tune:* La Donna e Mobile

I'm Nausea Bagwashio
Soap suds I sloshio
Give me your vestio
I'll do the restio
Why grow so weary
When for ten Lire
I'll be a wife and a mother-as-well to you.

Chorus: Be a wife dear, be a wife dear
And a mother-as-well
To you.

Niente mangario
Niente buvario
Oh niente vino
Niente icecreamio
Oh niente maidenhead
We have lost them all in bed
And the old Tedeschi† have taken them all away.

Chorus: The Tedeschi, the Tedeschi, etc.

I'm Nausea Bagwashio
I hate the Boshio
Their Passions I freezes
By giving them diseases
They gave me no restio
So I gave my bestio
And the old Tedeschi have taken it all away.

Chorus: The Tedeschi, the Tedeschi, etc.

Signalman Lampier

---

*When British troops invaded southern Italy in 1943, they were amused by the Fascist slogan 'Sempre Avanti!', meaning 'Always Forward!', which was written on the sides of buildings. They quickly crossed out 'Avanti' and substituted 'Indietro', meaning backwards; even the Italians laughed.
†Tedeschi means Germans; they were more commonly referred to as 'Teds'.

The ss *Askania* docked at Naples on 6 April 1944 and 'C' Battery had to clamber down ramps on to the horizontal side of a sunken hospital ship before they were able to put their feet on terra firma. Camped outside Naples for a few days, the Battery found the poverty and squalor of the population very depressing. 'Nausea Bagwashio' was certainly in her element! Across the Bay of Naples Monte Vesuvius puffed up smoke in a melancholy fashion. The Battery then proceeded to Piedimonte d'Alife, about 40 miles north of Naples, and by 16 April was reunited with its guns and vehicles. Here they continued their training and especially practised their drills of cooperating with tanks and infantry in close country.

It was not long before OP parties were sent to the area south of Cassino, where 12th Regiment was to be deployed in firing a massive barrage to support the attack of 13th Corps of the 8th Army, to which it now belonged. This attack was to coincide with other attacks on the Gustav Line by French and US forces to the south and the Polish Corps to the north. The latter's role was to outflank the Cassino Monastery position by a right hook through the mountains and then link up with 13th Corps in the Liri Valley. 13th Corps had been set a particularly tough task because it had to cross the River Gari, which lay across its front, before advancing up the Liri Valley along Highway 6. At the time of this attack the Germans had OPs on the high ground on both sides of the Valley and had

This map shows the area in which 12th Regiment fought from 11 to 29 May 1944. Regimental positions are approximate.

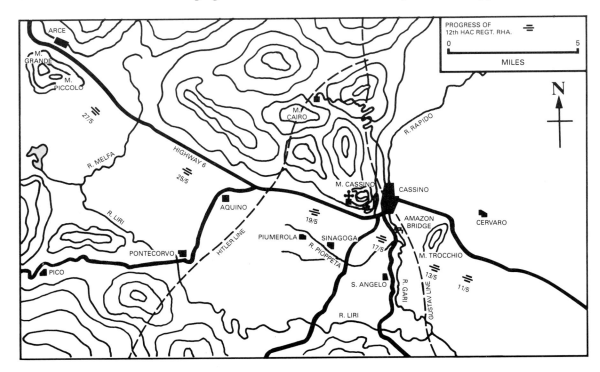

strongly fortified the thickly wooded and broken countryside with reinforced concrete positions, wire and mines.

In the initial stages 12th Regiment was to support 8th Indian Division as part of its fire plan, before reverting to its normal role of supporting 26th Brigade, who were temporarily with 4th British Division. The first task was to find suitable gun positions, which was not made any easier by the fact that all the obvious ones were already occupied. Nevertheless, Colonel Barstow and his Battery Commanders were able to find an excellent position in a little valley called Fosso del Lupo, to the rear of Monte Trocchio, which lay about four miles south-west of the ruined town of Cassino.

During the evening of 11 May the routine firing along the front line died down. Then at 2300 hours the Allied guns erupted in a massive barrage. On 13th Corps' front there were 1050 guns (compared with 882 guns at El Alamein). The noise of the bombardment was deafening and awe inspiring. The Germans at the receiving end thought so too, as a soldier on the Cassino Massif recalled:

> Suddenly, as if a light had been switched on, there was a blaze of flame down the valley ... and then ear-splitting screaming, whizzing, exploding and crashing. Splinters buzzed over me, stones and clods of earth whirled through the air. The ground trembled under the force of the blasts.[1]

There was not much light, though, from 12th Regiment's guns, which were using flashless propellant. Curiously, even in this cacophony of sound, men managed to hear the nightingales singing and noticed the beauty of the fireflies, which clung to their clothes and hair.

The Regiment went on firing at specific targets throughout most of the night. The infantry they were supporting had great trouble in crossing the River Gari, not only because of machine-gun, artillery and mortar fire but also because, when daylight came, visibility was limited by a natural fog, compounded by the smoke screen put down by both sides and the dust. These set-backs meant that the Regiment had to fire some of its fire plans again, especially repeating Target Spleen – the village of Castel St Angelo – until it finally fell on 12 May.

During the morning the OPs of 'D' Battery crossed the Gari on a class 40 Bailey bridge named Amazon, together with 2nd Lothian and Border Horse, to be followed by 'F' Battery OPs and 17th/21st Lancers. During this time 'C' Battery had a Priest hit by shell fire, but no casualties were suffered and the gun was soon in action again.

'C' Battery remained where it was until 13 May when, together with the rest of the Regiment, it moved up to the western slopes of Mount Trocchio. Later on that day it came under command of 26th Armoured Brigade again.

At first light on 14 May, 'C' Battery's OPs Major Rae, with Captain Austin-

Smith ('X' Troop) and Captain Atherton ('W' Troop), crossed the river with 16th/5th Lancers. The bridgehead they occupied was severely congested, with very little visibility and under continual, heavy enemy fire. Despite the overwhelming bombardment that 13th Corps had fired, the enemy's ability to retaliate was seemingly unimpaired.

> The German mortars were particularly difficult to suppress, for the mortar crews all had shell-proof dug-outs, and the mortars themselves were mostly sited in sunken roads or deep ravines where they couldn't be touched by a shell with an ordinary trajectory.[2]

So the 'C' Battery OPs were incarcerated in their tanks, which became increasingly like ovens as the day wore on; everyone was pouring with sweat and drinking as much water as they could. All the time they were under heavy fire. Nor did nightfall bring any relief as enemy mortar fire made it unsafe for anyone to sleep or eat outside his tank. They were lucky if they got as much as three hours' sleep. On the same day Gunner A. 'Sonny' Patching, who had the reputation of being a good boxer, and Gunner Herbert Mash were killed on the gun position.

Despite the determined resistance of the enemy, progress was slowly but steadily made up the Liri Valley. Captain Atherton was supporting 'B' Squadron 16th/5th Lancers and 6th Inniskilling. He knew that 'W' Troop had received some rounds of airburst and was determined to use them at the first opportunity. Here he describes that opportunity when it arose:

> Next morning [16 May] the ideal target appeared. The enemy were dug in, in trenches and emplacements, on the top of a bare grassy hill with no cover. The first ranging round of smoke fell plumb on, and the series of five airburst rounds from the ranging gun were just right – three airburst and two ground burst. The rounds of gunfire from the troop were concentrated and accurate. The result was devastating, and the noise was enough to make the stoutest heart quail, even from a few hundred yards away. Our infantry walked up and took the position without casualties.

For this action and his coolness and efficiency during the period 11–20 May, Captain Atherton was awarded the Military Cross.

On the evening of 16 May the Regiment fired a number of concentrations as the advance continued but was checked by a strong counter-attack by German parachute troops. This attack, it transpired, was to cover the withdrawal of the enemy from Monastery Hill. The Gustav Line had finally been broken. The valiant Poles had fought their way through the mountains round the notorious Monte Cassino and it was time for the Germans to withdraw to their next line of defence: the Hitler Line, 11 miles away.

The monastery of Monte Cassino can be seen in the upper right corner of the picture. This was the view of 19 May 1944 as it was seen by British troops who at last passed it. For the first time for weeks the monastery was clear of smoke screens. The advantage of the steep mountains both as OPs and lines of defence can easily be appreciated.

To the south, the French under General Juin brilliantly outfought the Germans in their fortified mountain positions and also broke through the Gustav Line, supported by the US 5th Army.

On 17 May OPs were able to bring down effective fire on the village of Piumarola, which was assaulted by the Skins 'with almost indecent rush'. They captured 100 German parachutists.[3] During that day the guns were moved across the River Gari from their positions on Monte Trocchio to new ones in an area where, only two days before, there had been heavy fighting.

On the following day the Regiment started to advance over pleasant rolling countryside dotted with orchards, white farmhouses and fields of green crops. By this time everyone had been told that Monte Cassino had fallen and they could see its ruined hulk over their right shoulders. Meanwhile the Derbyshire Yeomanry had come up to the Hitler Line at the town of Aquino. Here there was a pause as the guns of the Regiment tried to move forward at night along tracks already full of other units' vehicles. It was decided that the Hitler Line was too tough to be rushed and the Canadian Corps was brought up to make the breakthrough. This meant that after eight days of constant action and movement the Regiment was able to get some rest and clean itself up.

The Hitler Line was every bit as formidable as the Gustav Line and had been under preparation for the previous five months. The Germans were past masters at constructing steel and concrete gun placements and pillboxes defended by thousands of mines and wire. A novelty this time was a large number of Panther tank gun turrets armed with 88mm guns which had been taken off their chassis and embedded in concrete.

At 0630 hours on 23 May over 800 guns along the whole front opened an enormous barrage on the Hitler Line and by the next day the seemingly impregnable Line had been broken, with 'C' Battery's OPs advancing with 16th/5th Lancers again. The countryside they moved through showed all the signs of heavy fighting and destruction, including the depressing sight of numerous knocked-out Churchill tanks of the North Irish Horse.

> Every building, almost without exception, had been a target for a tank, a gun, a fighter bomber or an infantry assault … The Germans had evacuated all the civilians, leaving behind only the debris of the battlefield, the burned-out assault guns at the turn of a leafy lane, fields and orchards deeply rutted by scores of wheeling

A 105mm Priest self-propelled gun belonging to 12th HAC Regiment RHA advancing north of the River Gari on 18 May 1943. Note the 76 tactical sign used by all Royal Artillery units, the 0.5 Browning in the 'pulpit' and the unusual wireless arial.

Captain Mike Austin-Smith MC *who commanded 'X' Troop from August 1943 to April 1945. He later commanded 'C' Battery from 1952 to 1955.*

tanks, empty ammunition boxes, HQ sign boards, ration tins and cartons, helmets, German newspapers, gas masks and rows of newly dug graves.[4]

It should also be recorded that 'C' Battery's old Commander, Brigadier Clive Usher DSO and bar, now took over as CRA of 6th Armoured Division. His DSOs had been awarded in Tunisia and Sicily for his courage and leadership.

On 26 May 3rd Grenadier Guards, mounted on the tanks of 16th/5th Lancers, crossed the River Melfa but were checked by two hills – Monte Grande and Monte Piccolo – both about 1000 feet high and lying to the south of the town of Arce on the west of Highway 6. These hills blocked the advance of 26th Armoured Brigade, which tried unsuccessfully to work round the flanks. On the night of 27 May, 3rd Grenadier Guards took the summit of Monte Grande, but were forced to retire the next morning by determined counter-attacks made by the German 1st Parachute Division.

A little later Captain Austin-Smith was conducting a 'recce' in his Sherman down a narrow high-banked track, with Captain Eveleigh of the 16th/5th Lancers in front of him. Their directions were vague and Captain Eveleigh got out of his turret to get his bearings. He was promptly shot dead by a sniper and the next moment his tank was brewed up by a 'Panzerfaust'. Captain Austin-Smith immediately sprayed the banks with his Browning machine-gun and, taking on board the remaining crewmen from Captain Eveleigh's tank, backed up the track. His driver could not see properly because some camouflage netting had fallen over his periscope. However, after a while, they were able to turn round and regroup. For this action as well as for his gallantry, complete disregard for his personal safety, his cheerfulness and his offensive spirit, this popular officer was awarded the Military Cross.

While Captain Austin-Smith was extricating himself from this ambush, Major Rae, who had the knack of being in the right place at the right time, was able to bring down very effective fire to cover the Grenadiers' withdrawal and subsequently fired a number of 'Uncle Targets' on Monte Grande. In doing so he was later assisted by Captain Austin-Smith.

On their right, 2nd Coldstream had taken the summit of Monte Piccolo, but could not make any more progress because of heavy counter-attacks, some of which were broken up by the excellent shooting of the Ayrshire Yeomanry and the whole of 6th Armoured Division's artillery. Finally, the Monte Grande and Monte Piccolo positions were outflanked on the right by units of 8th Indian Division, and the Germans withdrew during the night. The fact that 1st Guards Brigade lost 18 officers and 265 other ranks killed and wounded during the three days ending 29 May gives some idea of the severity of the fighting.

After this battle the Regiment was able to rest and refit. It had taken part in an epic advance in which two extremely formidable lines of defence had been breached and the enemy were now retreating northwards towards Rome, where their flank was vulnerable to the Allied force which had broken out from the Anzio bridgehead. All the guns had fired an enormous amount of ammunition during this time. On the night of 11–12 May each gun fired at least 300 rounds, and again during the barrage on the Hitler Line on 23 May the allocation was 325 rounds per gun. During the period 12–18 May, 13th Corps artillery fired 476,413 rounds. As for 'C' Battery, their efforts were rewarded by not only both their Troop Commanders being awarded the MC but also their Battery Commander Major Rae. No doubt these awards reflected the skill, courage and determination of the individual officers as well as the support and efficiency of all members of the Battery.

From 29 May to 2 June the Regiment remained in the area west of Monte Grande, then on 3 June it moved a distance of 35 miles to a position west of Altari. The next day, 16th/5th Lancers with 'C' Battery took the lead and made good progress through valleys covered with orchards and vineyards. The latter posed a peculiar type of obstacle since the vines, which were strung on wires about turret height, could easily decapitate the unwary tank commander standing in his turret. To avoid this possibility the tanks drove deliberately at the vines, knocking them down in rows, much to the dismay of their owners.

At the end of this advance 16th/5th Lancers were held up by opposition some 22 miles east of Rome, at a village called Genezzano. Because of shell fire coming down on its right flank, 'C' Battery was forced to deploy in an extremely difficult and exposed position. This was accurately shelled with airbursts, and the GPO of 'X' Troop, Lt Eric Freeman, as well as Bombardier Wally Bennetts, Gunner A.H.M. Haynes and Gunner T.M. O'Brien were killed. L/Sergeant Farmer recalled comforting the dying Wally Bennetts, who talked of his family and home. He died in Farmer's arms, his wounds so extensive that Farmer was drenched in his friend's blood. Afterwards he had to change his uniform completely.

On the following day, 5 June, the American 5th Army entered Rome, to a tumultuous reception. The Germans were withdrawing to their next line of defence, the Gothic Line, which lay about 160 miles to the north and stretched from Pisa on the west coast to Rimini on the Adriatic. But the enemy were by no means routed and continued to fight with skill and determination, helped by the rivers and valleys which came down from the Apennines and presented obstacle after obstacle to the advancing Allies.

6th Armoured Division experimented as it went along, seeking the best tactical formation to use. As far as 12th Regiment was concerned, their problems were well explained by Lt Colonel Rae:

> At this point it might be advantageous to review the tactical considerations when siting guns in a moving battle. On this day [12 June], for example, 16th/5th Lancers were leading, with two Squadrons and a Regimental HQ – that is, about 36 tanks – on the road with 'C' Battery behind these and the reserve squadron behind 'C' Battery. Behind this party would be possibly Brigade HQ and Colonel Barstow, and behind that the guns of 'D' and 'F' Batteries. The information about the enemy is nil. It is known that they are somewhere ahead and until the enemy are contacted it is not possible to order guns into action.
>
> However, as soon as the leading Battery Commander has sufficient information to justify deploying his guns he will do this and the remainder of the Regiment will conform. The choice of ground for gun positions on these occasions is extremely limited, the guns cannot go back owing to the quantity of transport on the road and if they go into action too soon they cannot get forward along the road because of transport which has taken their place in the column. The same considerations apply to the two other Batteries in the line of march and it was these facts that caused the occupation of obviously indifferent positions on several occasions by all Batteries.[5]

The weather was hot now and the countryside was becoming more attractive – open and interspersed with woods. It was possible to enjoy the ripening fruit, especially cherries and mulberries. But it was certainly no picnic. There were constant problems to be overcome, from heavy traffic caused by other units to crossing rivers and coping with demolitions *en route*. The enemy, although retiring, were never far away and no one in 12th Regiment knew when they might come under fire.

On 15 June 16th/5th Lancers with 'C' and 'F' Batteries drove all night to take over the advance from the Lothians and 'D' Battery at Todi, 60 miles north-east of Rome on the road to Perugia. They were, in fact, travelling along the eastern bank of the River Tiber, whose western bank was occupied by the enemy. When 'C' Battery's position was shelled, one Priest was destroyed and some ammunition was set on fire. They suffered no casualties, unlike 'F' Battery, who lost three gunners killed and six wounded. By 20 June Perugia was taken and heavy rain prevented armoured vehicles operating off the roads. Here they stopped for two weeks.

This pause was forced on them not only by the weather but also because of the problems of bringing up supplies. In addition, the overall strategy of the war impinged itself on the situation. The Allies had successfully crossed the Channel and were fighting their way out of Normandy. There were, though, 40 divisions in the USA which could not be deployed in Normandy because of the shortage of harbours. It was therefore decided that priority should be given to a landing in the south of France to capture the port of Marseilles. For this purpose, General Alexander was asked to hand over three American and four French divisions. In exchange for these veteran formations he received the US 92nd Division – an Afro-American division – and a Brazilian infantry division. It was hardly a fair swap; the replacements were fewer in number and less experienced. This critically deprived General Alexander of the necessary strength to sustain his advance up through Italy. The remaining Allied divisions, including 6th Armoured Division, were left to fight their way northwards, becoming increasingly tired as the advance continued.

On 5 July they were off again, this time advancing in a north-westerly direction towards Arezzo, passing Lake Trasimene on their left. 16th/5th Lancers supported by 'C' Battery were held up by enemy fire three miles short of Arezzo. The next day the Derbyshire Yeomanry took over from 16th/5th Lancers, with 'C' Battery still in support. The Battery advanced about 1000 yards but came under such heavy observed fire that it had to withdraw, sadly not before Gunner J.A. Mease was killed and one Priest was knocked out.

The whole Regiment now took up a position near a house called the Villa Frasinetto and was heavily shelled during the next 10 days. Although strenuous efforts were made to reinforce slit trenches and command posts, the Regiment suffered another seven fatal casualties. But it was not all doom and gloom. On 12 July Captain Austin-Smith wrote home, explaining how much he had become part of 'C' Squadron of 16th/5th Lancers, who were very attached to 'C' Battery and 'X' Troop's Commander as well no doubt. He explained how they

won't budge an inch without their 7 (I'm always 7 on their net). Shells are referred to as 'grape' and Browning as 'Hotlead'. We have great fun on the net with whispered conversations such as 'Hot diggidy do give 'em some more hot lead' and

Tanks of 26th Armoured Brigade stopping on the road two miles north of San Benedetto, north of Florence, 20 September 1944. This type of mountainous country made it very difficult to find adequate gun positions.

'Bags of grape Mike, flush em out' and so on … We made up quite a good version of 'My Blue Heaven' when we were around the Hitler Line:

> When Squadrons all call
> And league is nigh
> I hurry to my old Sherman
> We tune to the news
> And I listen to Jive
> We're happy in our old Sherman
> You'll see a tiny space
> A dirty face
> And ---- all room
> A little brew that livens up

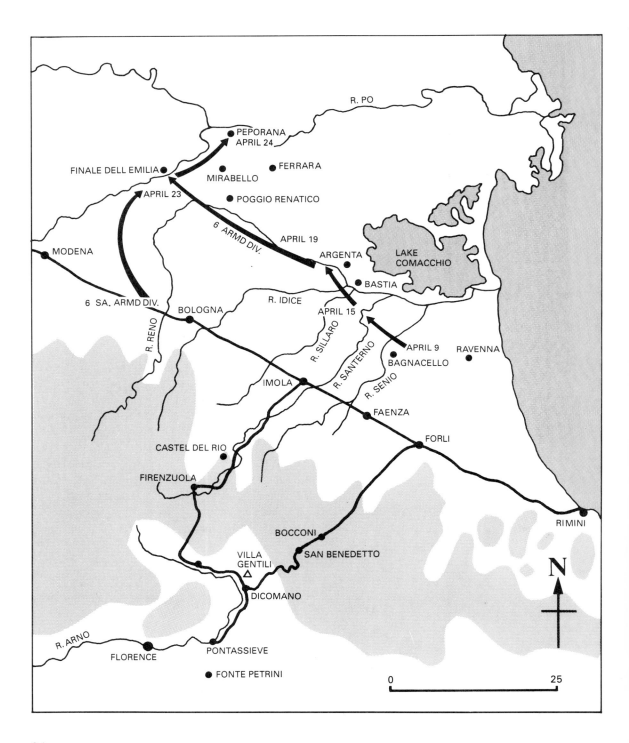

R. PO

PEPORANA
APRIL 24

FERRARA

FINALE DELL EMILIA

MIRABELLO

APRIL 23

POGGIO RENATICO

6' ARMD DIV.

APRIL 19

MODENA

ARGENTA

LAKE
COMACCHIO

BASTIA

6 SA. ARMD DIV.

BOLOGNA

R. IDICE

APRIL 15

R. RENO

R. SILLARO

APRIL 9

RAVENNA

BAGNACELLO

R. SANTERNO

IMOLA

R. SENIO

FAENZA

FORLI

CASTEL DEL RIO

FIRENZUOLA

RIMINI

BOCCONI

VILLA
GENTILI
△

SAN BENEDETTO

DICOMANO

R. ARNO

FLORENCE

PONTASSIEVE

FONTE PETRINI

N

0   25

The map shows the
area of operations in
the hills north of Flor-
ence from September
to November 1944
and the final advance
to the River Po in
April 1945.

Our long days of gloom
Just 7 and me
And Sunray* makes three
We're happy in our old Sherman.

The cause of 'C' Battery's uncomfortable sojourn at Villa Frasinetto was the fact that the enemy OPs on Monte Lignano could see into the gun positions only too well. Monte Lignano was one of a number of dominating heights that stretched across the front, south of Arezzo. The direction of the advance now moved again to the north-west and up the valley of the River Arno towards Florence. Here the country became more difficult for armour to move in; steep wooded valleys with mountain streams hindered their progress. OPs now found themselves having to leave their tanks to find decent points of observation on foot. The advance stuttered and started towards Florence. This city was evacuated by the Germans on 11 August and 6th Armoured Division pushed on to Pontassieve, about eight miles north-east of Florence, with their armoured regiments advancing in bounds towards the Gothic Line about 20 miles to the north. On 24 August the Regiment was visited by Major General Murray, the new Commander[†] of 6th Armoured Division, who gave a brief talk to all ranks.

The Gothic Line, although having few fortifications, was nevertheless a formidable obstacle. It consisted of blocked roads in narrow valleys overlooked by enemy infantry and their attendant OPs, who could bring down accurate artillery fire. The overall plan was for the US 5th Army to attack the Gothic Line along the west coast, for 13th Corps (containing 6th Armoured Division) to probe the centre towards Bologna, and for the 8th Army's 5th Corps, 1st Canadian Corps and Polish Corps to attack up the narrow coastal plain bordering the Adriatic towards Rimini and to try to turn the Gothic Line at that point. This they were able to do by pushing past Pesaro but after that they became bogged down in the marshy ground. To make things more difficult the rains started, and soft going became almost impossible.

Back now to 12th Regiment, who advanced slowly through the Apennines, still supporting 17th/21st and 16th/5th Lancers. Branching east of Dicomano, approximately 15 miles north-east of Florence, the Regiment found a position at

---

*Sunray means Commander.
[†]Major General H.B. Murray DSO had just taken over command of 6th Armoured Division from Major General G.W.R. Templer DSO, who had, in the short time he had been in command, greatly impressed the Division. Major General Templer had the misfortune of being injured by, of all things, a piano belonging to the Guards Brigade. The piano had been in the back of a truck which hit a mine just as it was passing the General's jeep. The piano sailed through the air and landed on the jeep.
History of the 17th/21st Lancers, R.L.V. Ffrench Blake, p. 188.

Major Michael Gilbert
CBE TD *who commanded 'C' Battery from September 1944 to October 1945.*
(Mark Gerson)

Villa Gentili, about five miles up the road. It was at this time that 'C' Battery lost its highly regarded Battery Commander Major Rae, who became Second in Command of the Regiment. Major Michael Gilbert, who took over in his place, had already established a reputation for daring and determination. He had been captured in Tunisia on 2 January 1943, when he was with 'D' Battery, and interned in POW Campo 49 in northern Italy. At the time of the Italian Armistice many prisoners were turned loose and, after walking about 400 miles, Major Gilbert rejoined the Allied lines in south Italy. For this he received a mention in despatches. Tall and bespectacled, Major Gilbert shared the same profession as his CO – he was a solicitor before the war – and his lively intelligence was happily linked to a dry sense of humour.

On 27 September the Regiment moved again, through the Gothic Line to San Benedetto, where they found it extremely difficult to locate decent gun positions off the road. Their efforts were aggravated by the steadily worsening weather. Rain turned small streams into roaring torrents and OPs in particular had a miserable time coping not only with the elements but also with accurate enemy fire. Life was not much easier for the guns, whose position could be reached only by tracked vehicles, jeeps or mules. Nevertheless, on 4 October they fired 250 rounds per gun to support an abortive attack by 7th Rifle Brigade.

After this, sufficient progress was made to advance up the steep side road to Bocconi. Forced to occupy the only possible area, the Regiment's gun position was well and truly registered by the German artillery.

On 7 October Captain Atherton became the Regimental Adjutant and Captain E.J.V. Williams took over 'W' Troop. On 16 October the Regiment handed over its responsibilities to its somewhat surprised friends, 17th/21st Lancers, who it was hoped would be able to hold their own with their new Sherman-mounted 105mm guns – a weapon they were never really very happy about. It was necessary for the Regiment to retrace its tracks and proceed via Dicomano and Firenzuola to Castel del Rio, which they reached on 17 October.

This new position was not much better than the last. The OPs continued to have a miserable time with restricted communications – line parties had to go out repeatedly to mend telephone lines which had been cut by shell fire.

By the beginning of November it became clear to everyone they would not be able to go any further; not only was the enemy defence resolute but the supply of ammunition had dwindled to 10 rounds per gun per day. This underlined the fact that 13th Corps, including 6th Armoured Division, had shot their bolt. All units were very tired and about 200 miles from the nearest railhead which prevented effective supply.

104th Regiment RHA took over 12th Regiment's position, with 'C' Battery moving back to Fonte Petrini, 10 miles south-east of Florence, to be joined by 'D' Battery 12 days later so that the Regiment was together again on 23 November. During the next week all its Priests and Shermans were handed over to Ordnance and the Regiment moved across the Apennines to Macerta, about 20 miles south-west of Ancona on the Adriatic Coast.

CHAPTER EIGHT

Grande finale in Emilia

The Army Commander has a craze for flexibility,
On his subordinates it lays a heavy strain.
Everyone must cultivate a passion for mobility,
'Wheels by road and tracks by train!'
Advance party forward. Rear party back.
(Chase the buggers round a bit to stop them getting slack.)
Seven days' rations. Everything's arranged.
Off you go! Back you come!
It's all been changed!

M.F. Gilbert

'C' Battery had been in action for six months and badly needed a rest and refit. Nevertheless, it was considered that, all in all, they had had an easier time than during their six months in Tunisia.

Conditions were more comfortable. There were, except in the latter stages, plenty of 'casas' [houses] for Command Posts etc, there was a reasonable amount of leave to very pleasant surroundings like Naples, Rome and Florence. Mobile cinemas were handy and mail and the *8th Army News* newspaper were regularly forthcoming. At no time did one really expect the enemy to attack and this knowledge enabled commanders to take risks in their forward recces and in their siting of gun positions without undue anxiety. The experience in Tunisia too, had been invaluable and the fact that everyone knew their job well made the tactical employment of each individual part of the Regiment a comparatively simple matter. Last but not least, there were no hostile aircraft.[1]

The facility of being able to take leave in civilized surroundings was, of course, much relished by everyone. The first leave parties went to Rome in August and later small numbers of officers and men got away to other cities as well. Regimental rest camps had been established in August at Arezzo and in October in the monastery San Domenica in Florence.

The delight of sleeping the whole night long in a warm bed between clean sheets can be appreciated only by those who have been denied that experience over a period of time. Apart from having fun as tourists, enjoying the 'vino' and the sights, including the girls with their dark voluptuous good looks, many men went to the opera. For many it was their first experience of this type of entertainment. It will probably not surprise the reader to learn that when that incurable romantic Captain Austin-Smith had spent three days' leave in Florence, he wrote home in a letter dated 9 November 1944:

The other day I saw the opera, the first time in my life I saw *La Bohème* and loved it, tomorrow I have a seat for *Rigoletto*, on Sunday there is *La Bohème* again, which I think I will see again.

On 2 December the whole Regiment moved again, squeezing itself into the small hill town of Monte Lupone. Right round the town was the old wall, in which were four huge gates. Monte Lupone was only 500 yards in diameter but somehow everyone was found a reasonable billet. The small theatre in the middle of the town was used for a regimental show on 23 December and then it was transformed into a dining hall for the Christmas dinner. There was excellent food – turkey, chicken, pork, stuffing, bread sauce, vegetables and Christmas pudding, all washed down with copious quantities of wine and spirits. After that the parties continued in the Sergeants' messes and individual billets until the early hours of Boxing Day. It was a memorable and happy time.

Shortly after Christmas the Regiment took delivery of 24 Sextons to replace their Priests. The Sexton had a 25-pounder mounted on a Canadian tank chassis called a Ram. There was much dismay about this change of gun: not only had the Priest proved itself a reliable vehicle but also its 105mm gun, with a heavier shell, was much appreciated. Its ability to fire airburst and a phosphorus shell for ranging was also a great advantage.

The necessary training for this new equipment did not prevent everyone enjoying New Year's Eve, as well as a marvellous party laid on in the theatre on 6 January 1945 for the local children, to which the entire Regiment had contributed their previous two weeks' sweet ration.

Towards the end of January it looked as if the Regiment might be recalled to Castel del Rio; such a prospect filled everyone with foreboding. But this order did not come about, although an advance party did go to Florence. Further orders and counter-orders were issued, and eventually the Regiment moved to the Florence area, their tracked vehicles going by train. The guns were calibrated at Pontedena near Pisa. Finally, the Regiment crossed the Apennines for the seventh time on 4 March and finished up at Pesaro on the Adriatic coast.

This fairly typical example of military chaos reminded everyone of other days at Thala, in Tunisia, and Ayr when the cry was 'haven't you heard, it's all been changed?' Although the exact reasons for this muddle are unclear, it was probably not unconnected with the fact that General Alexander, who was now Supreme Commander, had been instructed to withdraw from Italy 1st Canadian Corps and 200 US fighter bombers together with three British divisions from Greece and Egypt which had been earmarked for Italy, to fight in Germany instead. Churchill and the War Office had decided that it was on the western borders of Germany that the British forces should be strongest. Of course, this savage loss to 8th Army's strength meant a reshuffle of the pack, and new plans needed to be made if the intended spring offensive was to be successful.

During the month of March, the Regiment continued its training with the guns. The CRA Brigadier Usher inspected the Regiment and spent time talking to 'C' Battery, making sure he met those men who had not been in the Battery during his command.

Meanwhile, despite the problems of 8th Army's reduction of strength, plans were now well advanced for the final offensive. All units had been rested and reinforced, and enormous supplies of ammunition and bridging material had been stockpiled. New weapons had arrived to help with the battle. These consisted of flame-throwing Churchill tanks, known as Crocodiles; amphibious carrier tanks called Fantails; turretless Sherman tanks turned into troop carriers, called Kangaroos; and a host of other specialist engineering equipment.

During the winter the 8th Army's front line had slowly crept up to the River Senio, north of Ravenna (see map, page 84). They were faced by the German 10th

A Sexton 25-pounder self-propelled gun crossing the River Senio on a bridge consisting of two Churchill Arks on top of each other, 10 April 1945. The results of the previous bombardment can be seen on the flood banks, which were such a feature of this part of Italy.

Army, which consisted of seven divisions. These enemy troops had the advantage of defending the numerous rivers, canals and flooded areas which lay across the 8th Army's line of attack. The Germans dug their machine-guns, mortars and anti-tank guns into the dykes and tall flood banks which lined the water obstacles. The plan, code-named Operation Grapeshot, was for 8th Army to attack the Germans on the line of the River Senio and fight their way north to the River Po. Here they hoped to meet 5th Army, who would advance on 8th Army's left flank via Bologna. The two armies would attempt to surround the German armies south of the Po.

12th Regiment's role was to support 8th Indian Division, just as it had at Cassino, so on 2 April the guns moved to Bagnacallo, west of Ravenna. There, great trouble was taken to camouflage the guns and ammunition dumps in piles of wood and haystacks, or near farm buildings.

On 9 April the Regiment took part in a spectacular barrage which started at 1520 hours. Mike Austin-Smith described the attack in a letter of 27 May 1945:

We fired on the opening line +100 for 5 mins and then dropped 50 and five minutes later another 50 yds. This was to give the Air OP's time to correct us onto the actual banks of the Senio. We would fire about 80 rds grand then stop, this would be say at 15.50 when the Spits would swoop down and bomb and strafe the banks. This would last for ten minutes and at 16.00 the last Spit would climb up and away as all the guns roared out again. It was the most superb split-second timing and cooperation with ground and air forces I have seen.

This performance was repeated at intervals for 4 hours, all on the banks of the Senio. The noise was colossal, smoke and dust clouded the sky and the air was heavy with the smell of cordite fumes. The guns became terribly hot, the oil in the recuperators boiled and we had to keep a continuous supply of water at the guns to cool them off at every pause.

Water poured down the barrels, boiled immediately and they looked more like steam engines than guns. The afternoon wore on into the evening and H hour drew near. The guns paused and the Spits came roaring down in a mock attack as flame-throwing tanks crept up and flamed the banks. Orange, red flames seared the dust-laden air and at 19.20 the guns crashed down on the first line of the creeping barrage.

The sun was getting lower and the red rays of the sun accentuated the dust and smoke, making a savage setting for the blood-thirsty little Gurkhas to go into the attack. Within 20 mins we heard the banks were theirs, soon they had companies across, and while the guns blazed away until 23.30, round one had been won.

The next day, 10 April, the guns moved up to the River Senio and a 'recce' party was bombed by a group of 18 Allied aircraft. The Regiment lost one officer and four other ranks killed, and four men wounded. One of those killed was Gunner Young of 'C' Battery. In fact, it could have been worse, had the batteries moved up earlier.

Although they had had an exhausting 24 hours, everyone was in high spirits. The Regiment took part in another barrage during that night, firing on the Santerno, the next river line.

The advance continued in close country, making observation difficult, so a lot of shooting was done accurately to the map. The following day 'C' Battery crossed the River Senio. During the next three days the Regiment was able to rest and recuperate until it came under command of the New Zealand Division on 15 April, putting down a highly successful barrage for the crossing of the River Sillaro.

All this time the Battery wondered what had happened to 6th Armoured Division and what its role would be. Its men were no doubt happy to be reunited with 16th/5th Lancers and 26th Armoured Brigade on 19 April. Moving to positions north of Argenta, they fired coloured smoke to indicate a target for the bombers to attack.

Next day the three armoured regiments of 26th Armoured Brigade spread out with 16th/5th Lancers, supported by 'C' Battery, advancing about five miles. The flat country made soft going, and OP tanks which did not have Grousers* became bogged down under mortar and machine-gun fire coming from the high flood banks on their left flank. During this time the Regiment was allocated a flight of Air OPs.

> One aircraft was allotted to each Bty and worked on the Bty net, and owing to the close nature of the country did much shooting and registration which would have been out of the question for ground OPs. On one occasion two targets had to be registered quickly; it would have taken at least an hour to deploy a Tp Cdr so that he could see these targets. The Air OP was up and registered both targets at once in quick succession and later shot them with great success. All the pilots expressed great satisfaction with the accuracy of the Regt's calibration and the quick response they received.[2]

It was also on this day that an 88mm shell burst on the top of a bank through which Captain Austin-Smith's tank was passing. A number of shell splinters came into the turret, one of which hit his elbow and caused him great pain. He was quickly evacuated to a field dressing station and patched up before going on to hospital.

Lt R.D. Chudleigh took over 'X' Troop the next day, when the advance continued to Poggio Renatico with many Germans now surrendering. On 23 April 'C' Battery was still supporting 16th/5th Lancers, who advanced beyond Mirabello towards Finale Emilia. It was here, appropriately enough, that the Lancers met the leading units of 6th South African Armoured Division of 5th Army. The jaws had closed as planned and 14th Panzer and 1st Parachute Corps were doomed. Meanwhile, 'C' Battery fired on targets on the northern side of the River Po.

On 24 April the Regiment occupied a position at Peporana, just south of the River Po, hoping to be able to cross on bridges when they were built, but no orders came to move.

26th Armoured Brigade went on pursuing the enemy over the Po and were soon too far away for the guns to support them. 'The war has forgotten us,' noted the War Diary disconsolately, while Colonel Barstow fumed at not being able to be in at the kill.

'C' Battery had fired its last rounds in anger and eight days later, on 2 May, the war in Italy was over.

---

*Extensions to tank tracks, fitted to the existing tracks to give greater width and so better purchase.

CHAPTER NINE

Valiant hearts

Gladly they went to war because they knew
That hesitation would have brought the end
Of simple goodness which was their wish
As well as their high duty to defend.
So without further thought they took up arms
Nor laid them down till victory they saw –
And, evil being vanquished, then they said
'Henceforward let our enemy be war'.

Written, while at 121st OCTU, by
Captain Michael John Pugh RA, aged 24
Killed in Action in Italy, 3 June 1944

'C' Battery languished with the rest of the Regiment in a position just to the south of the River Po for nearly three weeks. They were unable to cross the Po for two reasons: first, an acute lack of bridging materials to build adequate bridges, and second, a shortage of petrol. Both these factors stemmed from the unexpected speed of the advance, which had outstripped the hard-working and often exhausted transport units.

On 2 May, when the news of the Victory in Italy Day was celebrated, a considerable supply of captured German Very lights contributed to an enormous fireworks display without causing too much havoc – with the exception of three small houses and a haystack! 'C' Battery quickly organized its social life by erecting a stage in a farmyard and putting up some coloured lights. They found a band of sorts from somewhere and the local village girls arrived to dance the night away.

In between these junketings, the Battery had time to think about the future. This time, unlike after the victory in Tunis, the whole war was almost over, and a feeling of insecurity and apprehension about the problems that peacetime might bring was in many people's minds. Gunner Thomas remembered thinking:

> In a short while the family I had known for six plus years would be scattered to the wind, and the idea of no longer belonging to 'C' Battery 12th HAC Regiment RHA, or indeed for that matter 6th Armoured Division, alarmed and disturbed me. Home was wherever the Battery was and in a short time it wasn't going to be anywhere.

It was scarcely surprising that everyone should wonder what the future held for them, since during the last 10 days both Mussolini and Hitler had died and the war in Germany itself was nearly at an end. It must have been the sudden speed of events that made everything so difficult for them to take in. In a special Order of the Day, Major General Murray, commanding 6th Armoured Division, tried to put the efforts of everyone in the Division into some perspective:

> The campaign in Italy is over. The battle lasted twenty-four days and resulted in the capitulation of all German forces in Italy unconditionally. This campaign, at a blow, completely destroyed an Army Group and caused the capture or destruction of about a million Germans.
>
> It is difficult for me to express in words the admiration I feel for the magnificent job which you have all done to make victory possible.
>
> The attack by 26th Armoured Brigade and the Derbyshire Yeomanry between 18 April and 23 April broke the German line on a twenty-mile front south of the Po and paved the way to the final victory ...
>
> Seldom in a campaign of the magnitude of the Italian campaign has one formation contributed in such great measure to final victory.

Our fighting qualities and our outstanding team work have made this possible.
It is indeed a privilege to command you.
Well done indeed, the 6th Armoured Division.
[Signed] H. Murray, Major General

But the success of 6th Armoured Division and the Allied armies was not without sacrifice. During the last part of the campaign, from April onwards, 8th Army had lost 7193 men killed, which was estimated to be about half of the German losses, without considering prisoners of war. The total Allied casualties for the whole Italian campaign were 313,495, of whom 119,279 were American and 89,436 were British. The German losses were in excess of 336,000.[1]

During the whole war, 12th Regiment lost 6 officers and 90 men killed in action, as the following table shows:

	Africa	Italy
Officers	3	3
Other ranks	41	49
	44	52

Total: 96

'C' Battery (included in the above figures)

Officers	–	1
Other ranks	14	13

Total: 28

On 6 May a special Regimental Service of Thanksgiving was held. Next day, orders came at last for the Battery to prepare to move. The guns were put on transporters and everyone else was to go on wheels to Velden in Austria.

The scenery in Austria was completely different from the Po Valley, with lush green grass, neat little villages and farmhouses on the Alpine slopes and the inviting waters of the Wörther See nearby. It was all very entrancing.

But there was work to be done. There were enemy arms and equipment to be collected; the whole area was awash with refugees, German army stragglers, deserters, SS men and Nazi Party officials – all had to be rounded up and sorted out; there were dumps of arms, food and clothing which needed to be found. 'C' and 'D' Batteries went to the village of St Veit to help with guard duties.

On top of all this, a serious situation was developing with the Yugoslavs. They had fought hard to liberate their country with the assistance of Allied personnel, weapons and equipment. In fact, they had been so successful that they had whole armies in the field and had invaded the eastern part of Italy, known as Venezia Guilia, whose principal port was Trieste. As soon as the Yugoslavs arrived they had set up a local administration, with hopes that by the time the 8th Army arrived they would find a New Yugoslavia already established.

All this was very unsatisfactory from the Allied point of view, since they had already agreed with Tito that they (the Allies) would occupy Trieste and use its port to provide the wherewithal for them to occupy Austria. It was therefore vital that both Trieste and the lines of communication were under Allied control. For a time there was a very real possibility that the Allies would have to impose their will by force, but in the end Tito's bluff was called and he agreed to the Allied demands. But it was touch-and-go for two or three days, and 'C' Battery might have found itself fighting the first battle of World War III.

Another problem, which has unpleasant repercussions even today, was the repatriation of Russian Cossacks who had fought for the Germans. The decision to return these wretched men was taken by Stalin and Churchill at the Yalta Conference on 4 February 1945. There was, though, a *quid pro quo* in this arrangement: it entailed the safe return of approximately 50,000 British and Commonwealth POWs who had been liberated by the Russians. 'D' Battery had to organize the accommodation of 3600 Cossack horses, and 'C' and 'F' Batteries helped to guard their previous owners before they were handed over by others to the Russians and an unknown fate. The horses were ultimately passed down the line but not before each Battery and RHQ had acquired 20 horses each.

On 23 May the Regiment found itself in the valley of the River Gurk, about 30 kilometres north of Klagenfurt in the Austrian province of Carinthia. 'C', 'D' and 'F' Batteries set up quarters in the villages of Strassburg, Gurk and Weitensfeld. Here they made certain they enjoyed the fruits of their victory. Although it was not Britain, this pretty Alpine valley must have seemed to some like paradise. When not on guard duty or patrol, officers and men learned to ride the horses and enjoyed all the sports and games they wanted, as Mike Austin-Smith wrote to his parents on 15 July 1945:

> Life has been so full these days. The last week or ten days have been simply terrific. We had our Regimental Gymkhana in which 'C' Battery won the shield, followed naturally by a jug-up. Then followed dinner parties, cocktail parties, race meetings, football matches, cricket matches, motorbike trials, more gymkhanas, more cocktail parties, dinners, football matches; all functions were held in superb surroundings and settings, with bands playing, and regimental tents with tables under coloured umbrellas; lunches of trout and raspberries and ice cream, wonderful houses on sloping lawns running down to mountain rivers, kilted pipers of the Gordons playing during cocktails and dinner served in marquees with coloured lights in the trees and around the swimming pool.

Most officers and men were able to go on leave in the UK and everyone was talking about the time when they would be demobilized. Some people enjoyed themselves so much they did not want to go away at all. The girls, with their fair complexions, were arguably prettier than the darker girls in Italy and immediately put the non-fraternization order under heavy strain. This order was in fact rescinded by the end of July 1945.

Towards the end of the summer it became clear that, like all good things, this happy time would have to come to an end. Lt Colonel Barstow, who had led the Regiment so enthusiastically during the last two-and-a-half years, went home to England on release. His place was taken for a short time by Lt Colonel Rae. In September, 11th and 12th Regiments HAC were amalgamated and when 'A' Battery of 11th Regiment merged with 'C' Battery 12th Regiment the wheel had turned full circle.

12th Regiment ceased to exist officially from 24 October 1945. As a regiment it had done everything asked of it with skill and courage, and had become an extremely efficient Royal Horse Artillery regiment. It had the good fortune to serve with 6th Armoured Division, who had also set the highest standards.

The British soldier has been eulogized by many people, who have mentioned his courage, endurance and discipline mixed with a unique blend of comradeship, gentleness and humour. All these qualities were to be found in abundance in 12th Regiment. But it was the Czechoslovakian leader Masaryk who, when broadcasting from London to his people just after the end of the Tunisian campaign, mentioned another endearing characteristic:

> I am grateful to the British soldiers – to those small humble citizens who are capable of being the greatest soldiers. But they do not talk about their deeds, they do not boast, and as soon as the war ends they will modestly disappear into their homes and cease to be heroes. Therein is their greatest glory.[2]

But it is right that the last words of this chapter should come, albeit unwittingly, from Gunner George Lamport of 'C' Battery. When asked by a friend what he was going to do after he had been demobbed, he replied:

> Oh, I shall go back to the Co-op. By this time next week I shall be back on my old milk round. All my customers will say: 'Where you bin George – on bleeding holiday?' – Suppose I have, in a way.[3]

CHAPTER TEN

'C' Battery at home

I saw a film today oh boy
The English army had just won the war
A crowd of people turned away
But I just had to look
Having read the book.

A day in the life
Lennon and McCartney

It is said that a country gets the government it deserves, and if this is true then it probably gets the army it deserves as well. At the end of the 1939–45 war, the Territorial Army was demobilized and the various regiments of the HAC were all in suspended animation. It was only in 1947 that the politicians, realizing that they did not have a large enough army to sustain their commitments in Europe or to maintain the crumbling bastions of Empire, decided to restore the Territorial Army and to initiate universal conscription with 18 months' National Service. The reestablished Territorial Army was to have 12 infantry and two armoured divisions, which was the same as in 1938.

This development should not have surprised anybody, since throughout the previous 300 years Britain had been raising and disbanding her armies and then raising them again, with a cheerful disregard for the lessons of history. During the following 25 years the British Army and its reserves experienced not only the rapid development of technological warfare, but also reflected the hopes and fears of society at large. By the time the Beatles were in full song in the 1960s their generation's perception of the army was completely different from that of their parents. Changes in technology and public attitude were to tug the Territorial Army, and the HAC in particular, this way and that as the years went by.

With the rebirth of the Territorial Army, the HAC was to raise an infantry battalion, an anti-aircraft regiment and a regiment of Royal Horse Artillery. Thus it was that on 1 May 1947 Lt Colonel Johnny Barstow DSO TD held his first parade in the drill hall (The Albert Room) at Armoury House for a unit called 235th RHA Regiment HAC. There were 13 officers and 13 other ranks present. It was not long before the Regiment's title was changed to 1st Regiment HAC, RHA and an HAC recruiting week was held within the City of London from 6 October to 10 October 1947. The results of this recruiting drive were disappointing, but despite the smallness of numbers, 'A', 'B' and 'C' Batteries were able to parade with a small but high-quality skeleton staff.

'C' Battery was commanded by Major Aubrey Lincoln MC, who was last seen as the Battery Captain in August 1943 before he was posted to 'B' Battery 152nd Ayrshire Yeomanry, which he commanded with distinction for the remainder of the war. Captain Mike Austin-Smith, now qualifying as an architect, also joined at this time as well as three other officers who had all been in the same Italian POW camp (Campo 49) – Captain Michael Gilbert, 'C' Battery's last wartime Battery Commander; Lieutenant Tony Davies, who had been an OP for 'F' Battery 12th Regiment when he was captured on that fateful night, 20 January 1943, on Point 286 near Bou Arada (see page 53); and Captain Peter Barshall.

Tony Davies managed to escape from Campo 49 at the same time as Michael Gilbert, but was wounded and recaptured just before he reached the British lines. Imprisoned in Germany, he escaped again, was recaptured and taken to

Prague, where he was released in 1945. Captain Peter Barshall had been a pre-war member of 'B' Battery HAC and had served in 138th Field Regiment RA under Colonel Clive Usher. He was captured but escaped from Campo 49 and succeeded in reaching Switzerland, whence he was finally able to return to England. The traditions of 'C' Battery were well cared for in the hands of these experienced and adventurous officers.

The criterion for joining 1st Regiment was that men should be aged between 18 and 40. Trained soldiers were required to do 30 hours' training a year (untrained soldiers had to do 40 hours) and everyone had to attend the annual camp for a period of between eight and 15 days. All members of the Regiment were required to be members of the HAC and if they had held a commission before they joined, they had to resign it and muster as a Gunner, although a number of people were quickly promoted again.

To begin with, all training weekends were held on a regimental basis. Members took part in firing royal salutes at the Tower of London. Weekend training

'Lest we forget!'
Roddy Hill-Smith,
Eddie Webb, Ken Rose
and John Bennett ('A'
Battery) salute the
Book of Remembrance
at Armoury House in
1948.

took place at Bisley in Surrey, where accommodation was available in the HAC's Bisley Hut. This building, which resembled a cross between a youth hostel and a shooting lodge, served as an excellent and convivial base for all types of military training.

'C' Battery's performance during the first year, although limited by lack of numbers, was nevertheless already reflecting the high standards for which the Battery had been known in the past, coupled with an exuberant love of life, qualities which could be described as not only working hard and playing hard but also doing whatever they did with style.

The first annual camp at Westdown on Salisbury Plain saw 'C' Battery getting its share of prizes. 'F' Subsection, consisting of Sergeant R.A. Wenham, Sergeant C.E.R. Francis and Gunners J. Fischal, H.K. Rose and W.P. Rosenberg, won the subsection prize. A composite Command Post team, consisting of Captain M. Austin-Smith MC, Gunners E.J. Webb and D.J. Webber, won the Command Post prize. 'C' Battery members also helped to organize a successful Flank Company's ball, and John Fischal was elected to captain the HAC's Rugby Club.

The final months of 1948 saw two important milestones in the Battery's history. On 5 October the first post-war battery dinner was held at Armoury House, with Major Aubrey Lincoln in the Chair welcoming his guest of honour, none other than Lt Colonel Clive Usher DSO, whom he described as the 'father of 'C' Battery'. Seventy-nine current and former members of the Battery attended, some of whom had not been seen since the early days at Borehamwood.

For the second event, 'C' Battery was able to muster enough men to man a four-gun troop to fire a royal salute at the Tower of London on 11 December 1947, to commemorate the accession of HM King George VI. They had the honour of being the first battery to do this since the war.

For the next 24 years 'C' Battery embarked on an annual round of training, which became routine as time went by, although there were developments and on occasions considerable variations. The season would start at the beginning of October with weekly training parades on Wednesday evenings. Two training weekends usually took place before Christmas at Bisley and on New Year's Eve a Batteries Ball was held at Armoury House. In the new year individual training proceeded and started to merge with training at troop level, assisted by probably two more weekends either at Bisley or further afield at Larkhill, when guns could be fired on a battery basis. Finally, the annual camp was the climax of the training year and lasted two weeks. A chronological list of 'C' Battery's Commanders and camps is printed on page 138.

The 1949 camp at Westdown was memorable: 'C' Battery put a skeleton battery in the field for a regimental scheme which was run on a two-battery basis, the second battery being provided by 'A' and 'B' Batteries with Captain Mike

Five past, present and future Battery Commanders can be seen here at the 1950 camp at Bodney in Norfolk. From left to right: Peter Barshall, Mike Austin-Smith, Tony Wenham, Aubrey Lincoln and Michael Gilbert.

Gilbert acting as their CPO. 'C' Battery was busy scoring points already and winning prizes as well.

In 1950 changes were afoot. First, Lt Colonel Barstow DSO TD handed over the command of 1st Regiment RHA to Lt Colonel G.R. Armstrong DSO MC TD. The latter had distinguished himself fighting with 11th HAC regiment RHA in the Western Desert and subsequently commanded 136th Field Regiment RA in Burma.

The second change was the announcement that, with effect from 22 June 1950, active units would be reinforced by National Servicemen who had completed their 18 months' service and were liable to do a further four years with the TA. The reason for this development was simply that the country was tired of war and not nearly enough volunteers had come forward to join the newly formed TA. 1st Regiment would have to wait until after the annual camp before the first conscripts joined them.

Although short of numbers, 'C' Battery was busy putting on the style. On 12 June 1950 the Battery held its first cocktail party, which became an annual event thereafter. The annual camp at Bodney in Norfolk was a successful one and the Battery boasted the highest percentage attendance. Apart from the officers, various personalities were establishing a reputation or notoriety for themselves. Three BSMs – John Keene, Roddy Hill-Smith and John Sewell MC (the latter had been with 11th HAC Regiment RHA) – had all made their mark. L/Sergeant Eddie Webb was first in the laying test. Eddie had joined 'C' Battery at the end of 1940 after his return from France via Dunkirk. He had served with the Battery throughout the war and his dedication, both military and social, was to continue for the next 13 years. John Attwood, a recent recruit, also was hard to ignore, not only because of his height but also his enthusiastic behaviour!

In the autumn of 1950 the National Servicemen came flooding in and it was possible to establish two proper troops – 'Easy' and 'Fox'. The first National Serviceman to join the Battery was Gunner R. Oakes who no doubt arrived in

time to take part in the off-season reunions which were held during the summer. These were known as TEWTs (Tippling Exercises With Tankards) and took place in a variety of pubs, usually between Belgravia and Kensington. The Grenadier, Nag's Head, Antelope, Admiral Codrington, Bunch of Grapes, George IV and Windsor Castle on Camden Hill were all popular watering holes. Their popularity came and went, not least when the Battery found itself banned from one or another for a period of time.

The 1951 camp at Tilshead Lodge on Salisbury Plain saw the Battery with 146 officers and men on parade – a big difference from only 45 officers and men who were at camp the year before. The numbers were made up not only by National Servicemen but by regular reservists, known as 'Z' men.

Although camp was the military climax to the year, 'C' Battery, which never seemed to miss an opportunity to have a party, decided that a battery dinner and cocktail party were not enough and accordingly organized its own dance at Armoury House on 9 November 1951. Three hundred people attended this new event in the London social calendar and danced to Sydney Lipton's Band with much enjoyment.

Three weeks before the dance the Battery, now at almost full strength, had a training weekend at Bisley. 'On this last occasion the Saturday evening session in the Hut reached unparalleled heights of voodooistic frenzy. Mr Daniels [the Manager of the Hut], handed the Major [Lincoln] his early cup of tea on the following morning with the stark utterance "Your Battery, Sir, isn't human!"'[1]

1952 saw a change in command. Major Aubrey Lincoln MC was promoted to

1951 camp at Tilshead Lodge on Salisbury Plain saw 'C' Battery commanded by Major A.G.P. Lincoln MC TD with a record 146 officers and men on parade. The majority of these were National Servicemen and 'Z' men.

Champagne Charlie. In the summer of 1957 several members of 'C' Battery visited another member, Jock Ennis, who was working for six months for the House of Mercier at Epernay in France. As a result of this visit, Monsieur Jacques Mercier was invited to watch 'C' Battery fire a Royal Salute at the Tower of London in February 1958. He is seen here talking to (from left to right) Bombadier David Girling, RSM R.S. Page, BSM Eddie Webb and Captain Derek Walker. Later they returned to Armoury House to drink a case of Extra Dry kindly given by Monsieur Mercier, who remarked that, in his experience, 'Les Artilleurs ont toujours soif'.

Second in Command of 1st Regiment and Major Mike Austin-Smith MC took over the command of 'C' Battery.

Many sports were popular with members of the Battery. As the years went by, many of them played rugby, soccer, hockey or cricket for the HAC, although not always with the first team. These sports presented an excellent opportunity to meet other members of the HAC, in both the batteries and the Infantry Battalion. They also produced a number of recruits from opposing teams. In the summer of 1952, at a Batteries *v* Battalion cricket match, 'C' Battery had its own marquee, produced by Jim Wilson the Quartermaster and erected by Derrick Walker and friends. On another occasion the Battery played cricket at Luddesdown as guests of Michael Gilbert. 'That we were defeated is due largely to the treacherous behaviour of Wilfred Picton-Turbervill, who turned out for the home side.'[2]

105

And so the years went by, although it would be difficult to add 'with monotonous regularity', as far as 'C' Battery was concerned. The characters who had started the Battery had attracted others of a similar bent and although people came and went, there was always a core of people who generated an infectious enthusiasm. One such character, Geoffrey Posner, organized a visit to see the farce *Dry Rot* at the Whitehall Theatre. 'The only thing dry about this was the name. We started in the pub, the play took place in a pub and we finished in a pub. This is the perfect recipe for a 'C' Battery entertainment.'[3]

It was at the 1955 camp that Major General Dawnay visited the Battery during its fire and movement exercise. He wished to speak to everyone on the guns individually and, taking him at his word, Bob Elphick introduced his subsection as 'My No. 3 Nigel Brook, my No. 2 David Kahn...' Then he realized his ghastly breach of military etiquette and finished, in a cold sweat, with the words, 'Stokes, my No. 4'.[4]

Despite all this nonsense the Battery soldiered as hard as it played, capturing the Regimental Signals prize (Michael Charlesworth) and the Command Post prize, in which John Fairbank scored 100 per cent in the Command Post Assistant's prize. The camp in 1956 was the first one at which the Regiment had towed guns and given up their Sextons which they had enjoyed so much.

There were changes in command as well. In 1955 Major Mike Austin-Smith MC took over the command of the Regiment from Lt Colonel Aubrey Lincoln MC. Thus 'C' Battery had contributed two consecutive Commanding Officers of the Regiment. It is pertinent to say how much both 'C' Battery and 1st Regiment owed to these two officers, who had imbued everyone with the Royal Horse Artillery spirit of going flat out at whatever they undertook.

The source of most of the information in this chapter is, of course, the 'C' *Battery Notes* in the HAC *Journal*. It is timely, though, to note that 12th Regiment was meeting regularly for reunion dinners once a year at Armoury House. They came from all corners of the land to meet each other and to renew old friendships. The batteries dined together at their own tables and many were the memories they recalled.

Memories were also brought back when an official visit was made to Tunis to attend the war graves dedication ceremony at Medjez-el-Bab in November 1957. This visit was notable not only because of all the feelings it must have stirred up but also because the winter rains started early and literally swamped the expedition. Both Colonel Aubrey Lincoln and Mrs Diana Barstow wrote accounts for the *Journal*. Mrs Barstow wrote:

The Military Cemeteries are of dignified design and perfectly maintained by the Imperial War Graves Commission. The stone used is a soft pale sand colour. The cross which dominates each one rises slenderly from a background of cypresses. At

'Cocktails and laughter, but what comes after?' It was the custom of the Battery to meet up for impromptu parties after the end of camp each year. This picture was taken in the summer of 1957 at the Blue Angel in Berkeley Street W1. From left to right: Trevor Tyler, John Chandler, Michael Scrivener, Mike Cockell, Aubrey Lincoln, Derek Walker and Brian Brockman (Royal Marines).

Medjez it is flanked by pergolas linked by a wall. At the end of each pergola are stone pillars on which are carved the names of those who fell in battle and whose bodies were not recovered. The grave stones are simple, each one carved with the soldier's regimental crest and his name.

At the bottom of many stones is a message chosen by the soldier's relatives, touching reminders of individuality.[5]

In 1959 'C' Battery was the first battery to put six guns into the field. The Battery strength was over 100 but they were unable to practise their gunnery at camp because 1st Regiment had to spend a fortnight learning the art of civil defence at Penell's camp, near Merstham in Surrey. Although everyone tackled the training with typical enthusiasm, no one was really happy without their guns. This did not stop anyone from enjoying themselves and relishing some of the new techniques they learned.

We also learned how to bandage and splint, and to rescue casualties from heights and voids using only ladders, ropes and stretchers. John Attwood gave a sustained performance as a wounded husband under a floor, who gallantly insisted that his 'wife' should be rescued first. This continued until what we thought was his 'wife' in fact turned out to be Roddy Playfair holding a piece of his 'wife's' most intimate clothing.[6]

107

It was therefore not until 1960 that 1st Regiment were able to practise their six-gun battery techniques at the annual camp at Sennybridge, where it rained for a lot of the time, as it usually does. It was the last camp for Colonel Mike Austin-Smith in his role as Commanding Officer, and he impressed everyone by jogging around the Battery's gun positions in the early morning. 'C' Battery, who never believed in roughing it any more than it had to, had brought along a generator to provide electric light.

The Sutling Tent did considerable business, ably backed up by the hotdogs cooked in a bright blue (non-tactical) fish-and-chip van, which Clifford Coxe had found and which he towed all the way from London and back again. The Sutling Room (which became a tent at camp) is a unique feature of the HAC. Normally when the HAC is using its headquarters at Armoury House it does not have an Officers' Mess. This phenomenon only appears at camps or on active service. In Armoury House there is one bar, known as the Sutling Room, where all ranks drink and intermingle. A male preserve, it originated in days gone by when officers were elected by the votes of members. It was usually found that at camp not many officers used their Mess, except for dining, and quickly made their way to their own battery's Sutling Room.

During the 26 years of 'C' Battery's post-war existence there were probably two really exceptional annual camps. These were the 1961 Round Britain camp and the 1970 camp in Cyprus. The idea of the Round Britain camp was possibly inspired by 12th Regiment's movements in the UK in 1941 and 1942, when it finally marched to Ayr in Scotland. In 1961, instead of staying at one location, 1st Regiment picked up its guns and equipment at Thetford in Norfolk and drove via Salisbury Plain to Sennybridge, and thence onward to Otterburn in Northumberland via Bickerton in Cheshire. 'C' Battery could not deploy its fish-and-chip van that year. Instead, it brought a blue Sutling Tent of its own (which was arguably more useful).

The first days of the camp were greeted by glorious sunshine. The drive in convoy to Larkhill on Salisbury Plain was uneventful and the Battery trained to compete for the Jock Cup (a 'quick action' competition named after Jock Lovibond, who had been 11th Regiment's Medical Officer at the outbreak of war and had remustered in 1947). The Battery practised numerous gun positions:

> 'Action Front!', gun out – on to platform – uncouple. Turn to 'front'. Sights into bracket. Block scale angles out. Survey point and distant object. Aiming posts out. Slipping scale angles out – near and far objects. Clinometer angles. Range. 'Load', 'Fire'.[7]

So went the drill but, despite 'C' Battery's best endeavours, 'A' Battery won the Jock Cup that year. 'The reasons why we did not win were variously explained – the Guns blamed the Command Post, the Command Post the OP and Tony Wenham blamed everybody.'[8]

When the Battery arrived at Otterburn it prepared itself for the BRA's three-day exercise:

> This started punctually next morning with a downpour of rain, which lasted nearly all the time and was memorable for an attack by a Geordie parachute unit, which

ended with their having to ask for the return of their captured rifles. Morale was extremely high throughout the whole exercise in spite of wet camouflage nets which considerably added to our discomfort. The Gunners, not to be outdone by the Officer's guest night, celebrated in their inimitable fashion at the end of this exercise.[9]

It was a very good and unusual camp, and although 'C' Battery did not win the Jock Cup, it won its fair share of the various regimental trade tests and competitions:

> The Battery won the Command Post prize. Gerry Tapson, Ian Skews and Donald Biddle came first, second and equal fourth in the Detachment Commanders' tests. John Swain came first in the Gunners' RHA test and David Clarke second. David Young came second in the Signallers' test. Guy Edmunds received the Battery Commander's prize.

After this camp Major Tony Wenham handed over the command of 'C' Battery to Major Brian Davis. Tony Wenham had commanded the Battery for five years with skill and a flamboyance which was never flashy. His successor Brian Davis was thoroughly committed to the HAC and naturally to 'C' Battery. His ambition was to see the Battery reach new heights of performance.

In the year 2000 a social historian looking back at the preceding hundred years may well consider that 1960–69 was the most enjoyable decade of the century. Britain had shaken off the austerity of the 1950s (food rationing had finally ended in 1954) and the last National Serviceman was called up in 1960. Also at this time the HAC had reverted once more to relying on volunteers rather than reservists.

As the army's commitments changed and the Cold War intensified, so it was necessary to review the role of the Territorial Army. The HAC's role came under close scrutiny and after much negotiating it was agreed that the main role of both the 1st Regiment HAC, RHA, and 1st Battalion HAC was to produce a reserve of potential officers. This meant the establishment of an Officers' Training Wing.

The social historian might ponder what manner of young men volunteered to join the HAC at this time. In the period 1 November 1947 to June 1964, 1776 new members were admitted to the Company's membership. In the main they were pursuing professional or commercial careers in the City of London and its environs. They were well educated but not exclusively so – only three out of 10 had been pupils at the top 20 public schools. In August 1964 the HAC *Journal* published a table of those schools where members had been educated. The following table shows the most popular schools as far as 'C' Battery members were concerned, for the period December 1954 to December 1964. The figures in brackets indicate the position in the HAC's overall listing.

ABOVE: *Winners of the Queen's Cup 1962. Major Brian Davis TD is Battery Commander.*

BELOW: *'C' Battery Dinner 13 October 1988. One hundred and thirty members and guests dined at Armoury House in anticipation of the Battery's 50th anniversary. Amongst those present were nine members who joined in 1939, five Battery Commanders and six Regimental Colonels.*

OVERLEAF: *Salute at the Tower of London. 'C' Battery HAC, RHA, commanded by Major B.C. Bicknell TD HAC, firing the Royal Salute at HM Tower of London, 2 June 1971.*

ABOVE: *Major Tony Wenham* TD *(left) giving orders to Lt John Fairbank before a Salute at the Tower of London circa 1960. Major Wenham commanded 'C' Battery from 1957 to 1961.*

LEFT: *(From left to right) Captain John Chandler, 2nd Lt Peter Smith, Major Brian Davis* TD *who commanded 'C' Battery between 1962 and 1966, and Captain Mike Liscombe (RAMC).*

'C' Battery 1954–1964

		School attended	No. of members
1	(1)	Wellington	11
2	(11)	Downside	8
3	(13)	Radley	7
3	(9)	Uppingham	7
5	(4)	Harrow	5
5	(7)	Rugby	5
5	(20)	Stowe	5
8	(2)	Marlborough	4
9	(3)	Haileybury	3
9	(5)	Tonbridge	3
9	(18)	Ampleforth	3
9	(20)	Shrewsbury	3
			64

Of the remaining 73 members, the majority had been to various other public and independent schools and only 13 to grammar schools. Thus it was apparent that nearly half (47%) of 'C' Battery's intake came from the better known public schools as compared with the HAC's overall average of 30%. These were the years before the expansion of tertiary education and only 18 of the total of 139 men had been to university. Three of these had been to Peterhouse, Cambridge, and all of them served the same gun! Eleven of the others had been to Oxford. It would, however, be wrong to read too much into these figures. The common denominator of all members of the Battery, and indeed of the HAC as a whole, was the desire to serve their country and enjoy good comradeship within a military context.

The years 1962 and 1963 saw 'C' Battery twice representing 1st Regiment in the Queen's Cup competition, a fire and movement exercise similar to the Jock Cup. It was open to all gunner regiments in the TA. In 1962 the Battery started training for this event at the end of August, a month earlier than usual. Training was intense and sober (by 'C' Battery standards) and the result was the Battery lost, beaten by 359th Medium Regiment from Liverpool.

In the following year the Battery actually won the Jock Cup at the annual camp at Westdown for a change. For the second time 1st Regiment qualified for the finals of the Queen's Cup, and 'C' Battery was again in the hot seat, hoping to justify itself after its failure the previous year. On 22 September the Battery was put through its paces and beat the keen competition provided by 252nd (Manchester Artillery Regiment) RA (TA) and 851st (Westmoreland and Cumberland) Independent Battery RA (TA). A month later 1st Regiment mounted a guard of honour and 'C' Battery was hospitably received by the Lord Mayor, Sir Ralph Perring, whose son Richard was happily an officer in the Battery. Major Brian Davis received the Cup from Her Royal Highness Princess Alice, Countess of Athlone.

As well as rushing round the UK and winning glittering prizes, 'C' Battery had been applying its surplus energy to finding other ways in which to enjoy itself. One popular development was a battery motor rally, which in the late 1950s was successfully organized by Adrian Platt and David Crothall. Another was the formation of 'The Syndicate', consisting of Clifford Coxe, David Young, John Fairbank and James Longcroft. 'The Syndicate' made its first appearance at the camp at Tilshead Lodge in 1962, suitably dressed in dinner jackets. Punters were invited to play roulette or chemmy in the *salle privée*, where there was free champagne. That year the Sutling Tent was run by Adrian and Christopher Rowbotham and Robin Widdows, dressed in black ties, white shirts, stable belts and patrols.

In 1964 and 1965 the now well-established routine pursued its annual round and although stalwarts of the Battery retired, such as BSMS Douglas Garland and Eddie Webb and BQMS Guy Edmunds, their places were filled and it must have seemed that the 'C' Battery show would run forever. Little did anyone guess that their world was about to fall apart.

CHAPTER ELEVEN

Last post

Almighty God, whom to serve is perfect freedom,
and by providence the Honourable Artillery Company
has proudly fulfilled its citizenship in the ancient
capital of our land; grant that, armed with the shield
of faith and the sword of the spirit, we may serve
thee in freedom and peace as citizens of that
other realm of which our Saviour Christ is Lord
of Lords and King of Kings.

The Rev. C.E. Leighton Thomson TD
Regimental Collect of the Honourable Artillery Company

The year of 1966 started for 'C' Battery in tragedy and, some would say, ended in farce. The tragedy occurred on 12 February in Derbyshire when the Battery Captain, Captain John Fairbank, and Gunner Peter Ashcroft were hit by a car while they were walking down a road during an adventure training weekend. Both Captain Fairbank and Gunner Ashcroft were taken to hospital, where the latter recovered, but Captain Fairbank died two days later. For any man to die in his prime is of course a tragedy for his family and his friends, but John Fairbank was a particularly talented and much loved man and so his death seemed doubly sad. He had joined the HAC in 1951 and was the epitome of what an HAC officer should be. He was an actuary by profession and was accordingly fascinated by the mathematics of gunnery.

> His zest and enthusiasm were infectious: he could never maintain for long the mock pompous pose he loved to adopt: the facade would soon crumble into that explosive chortle which was very much his own.[1]

There seems little doubt that had he lived he would have commanded not only 'C' Battery, but the Regiment as well.

The annual camp was held at Sennybridge and was the last one at which Major Brian Davis commanded the Battery, because he had been promoted to be Second in Command of the Regiment. He had commanded the Battery for five years with dedication and enthusiasm and had not only maintained its spirit but increased its efficiency. It was a difficult time for the HAC though, as there were major changes on the way.

The Government had decided to reorganize the Territorial Army as a result of an appraisal of the role of the Regular Army. It was argued that it would be likely that if a European war developed, it would be nuclear in character. The result of this thinking was the reorganization of the reserve forces into an Army Volunteer Reserve. The role of the HAC was changed to put more emphasis on officer production and training.

There was only room for one battery of artillery. This was made up from 'A' and 'B' Batteries, and some men from 'C' Battery – it must have looked at one time as if 'C' Battery itself would be disbanded. However, 'C' Battery and a company from the Infantry Battalion were transferred into a strange hybrid called the Greater London Regiment, which was part of AVR III (Territorials). This Regiment was based at Tower Hamlets[2] and was to assist the civil power in times of emergency and also to provide a civil and home defence capability. Thus was 'C' Battery deprived of its traditional role of an RHA battery and reduced to being no more than a unit of the Home Guard, guarding vulnerable points, as it had in 1939.

It was a time of crisis and although 'C' Battery was determined to do its duty, there must have been a real feeling of dismay. It is at times like these that the need for strong leadership is paramount. In view of Major Davis's promotion it was necessary to appoint a new Battery Commander. The officer who took over was Major Graeme Gilchrist, who had served in 'G' Locating Battery of HAC, and his appointment could not have been a happier choice. He was an intelligent and natural leader blessed with a sense of humour and the ability to get the best out of individuals, some of whom had come from his old Battery. He was certainly fortunate in having Captain David Young and Lt Clifford Coxe, both of whom having already contributed so much to the persona of 'C' Battery.

Training in 1967 started on 5 January and drill nights were held on alternate Thursdays. It was important that the Battery involved itself in as many activities as possible. Thus a 'C' Battery team of eight came second in the TA Eastern Command Cross-Country Championships and first in the 56th East Anglian Brigade Championship. On 21 April the Battery exercised its role as a member of the HAC and fired a salute at HM Tower of London, thereby maintaining its old Gunner tradition.

The annual camp was held at Folkestone and the Battery was trained in an infantry role by the 1st Battalion Staffordshire Regiment. The camp started with an inaugural parade. At the rehearsal for this parade the RSM explained to everyone that they would be inspected by the GOC Southern Command, Lieutenant General Sir David Peel-Yates, and as far as they were concerned he was the equivalent of God Almighty. At this a voice from the rear rank of 'C' Battery was heard to say: 'He may be God Almighty to you, but he's Uncle David to me!'

'C' Battery did everything it could to adjust to its new role and because of strong leadership and the inherent loyalty within the Battery, it succeeded beyond reasonable expectations. The fact remained though that the experiment of AVR III was not working. There was friction with the management and in retrospect the idea of being able to sustain interest and enthusiasm for training for such an ill-defined role was extremely optimistic.

The Government was also having second thoughts. Because of a financial crisis, no one in 'C' Battery was paid during the period from July 1967 to December 1968. The Battery therefore found itself in limbo, but resolutely refused to give up. Major Gilchrist, by dint of much lobbying and cajoling, was able to arrange for the Battery to attend a week's camp at Sennybridge at the end of June 1968. Out of a strength of 76, 42 officers and men attended this camp and did not receive a penny for their enthusiasm. It was an astonishing effort and if it ever needed to be proved that the 'C' Battery spirit was not based on gin and tonic, this response would clearly satisfy any doubters. Major Gilchrist received considerable support at this time from Captain Basil Bicknell, who had taken over from Captain David Young on his retirement. Another officer who generously gave his time to help the Battery was the Adjutant, Captain Bill Hebblethwaite RHA.

'C' Battery camp, 1969, at Rollestone. Battery Commander Major Graeme Gilchrist TD.

Because 'C' Battery only existed on paper, they were not only unpaid, but far more importantly they had no call on artillery equipment or guns. These basic necessities were met by joining forces with the Oxford University Officer Training Corps and also by the generous assistance of 'A' and 'B' Batteries HAC, who provided essential equipment. Thus it was that the Battery was able to man four guns, whose No. 1s were Sergeants Mike Stewart, Peter Corke, Tim Livingstone-Booth and Lt David Snell of the OUOTC. The OPs were manned by Major Gilchrist and Captain Bicknell. Lt David Healey was the GPO. Although 'C' Battery's camp lasted for only a week and despite the fact that only half the Battery had actually fired a shot, they quickly attained a very high standard of gunnery. This was not achieved without the usual conviviality of the Sutling Tent. As usual funny stories abounded, as did the number of dogs belonging to 'C' Battery members.

On one occasion Gunner Derek Wood was observed by the RSM exercising Captain Bicknell's dog, Hac. The RSM told him to keep in step. 'After a long pause, the Senior Gunner replied, "I can't, Sir, he's got four legs and I have only got two."'[3]

After this camp training limped along until the 'C' Battery dinner at Armoury House in November. It was then that Major Gilchrist made a particularly memorable speech in which he vigorously emphasized the importance of the armed forces in an uncertain world, quoting a speech made by Winston Churchill in 1904:

The Army is not like a limited liability company to be reconstructed, remodelled, liquidated and refloated from week to week as the money market fluctuates. It is not an inanimate thing like a house, to be pulled down or enlarged or structurally altered at the caprice of the owner or the tenant, it is a living thing. If it is harried it gets feverish; if it is sufficiently disturbed it will wither and dwindle and almost die.

116

Whether his stirring words had been heeded by those in authority or whether it was a happy coincidence, when the Battery met to dine at the Bisley Hut a month later they were told by Colonel Brian Davis (now commanding the Regiment) that with effect from 1 January 1969 'C' Battery was to be reestablished as a third battery of the HAC. After two years in the wilderness the Battery had come home.

The 1969 camp at Rollestone saw 'C' Battery borrowing guns from the Cambridge University OTC. Once again it was only able to train for a week, but despite its comparative lack of training it did very well to come second to 'A' Battery in the Jock Cup, especially since 'A' Battery had competed at the end of their two-week camp. This was the last camp at which Major Graeme Gilchrist commanded 'C' Battery. He was subsequently promoted to be Second in Command of the Regiment. There can be no doubt that he had done a remarkable job commanding 'C' Battery during a most difficult and taxing time in the Battery's history. His place was taken by Major Basil Bicknell. Under its new Commander, 'C' Battery would certainly not be allowed to change its style, for Major Bicknell possessed great energy and a selfless devotion to the Battery and the HAC.

'C' Battery was now able to settle down to a proper training year, which finished with the annual camp in Cyprus. The Infantry Battalion had enjoyed a camp in Malta in 1966, but with the exception of small numbers of officers and men who had taken part in NATO exercises and training weekends in Germany, 1st Regiment had never taken on an overseas assignment. The camp was arranged at very short notice. All concerned had to pay their own fares on Dan Air charter aircraft. The Regiment travelled in mufti because an election involving Archbishop Makarios was about to take place and the political situation was particularly sensitive.

After a delayed start from Gatwick, which presented a good excuse for an impromptu sutling party, the aircraft finally landed at Nicosia with some people on board extremely hazy about how they had got there. Sergeant Peter Corke in particular made a memorable entrance into the airport buildings, and next day Gunner Corke found himself on a parachute training course.

The only guns available were 81cm mortars, so the Regiment had to carry out a course of infantry training. Because of the heat, training was carried out only in the mornings, with Reveille at 0400 hours. 'The GPMG, SLR and SMG were all duly fired, the latter with deadly accuracy from the hip to the amazement of a visiting UN contingent.'[4] Grenade throwing proved to be an exciting exercise, especially for Bombardier Geoffrey Godbold who rashly advanced to resurrect his target when he heard the immortal words 'Ready, throw' from the instructor to the next thrower. 'Never has a man turned more quickly on a sixpence and dived headlong into the shelter.'[5]

Mortar practice was particularly enjoyable until someone tried firing one

horizontally. Needless to say, the time needed to recover from these adventures was well spent. A regular Pimms party, masterminded by Captain Clifford Coxe, meant that by the end of camp there was not a full bottle left on the island. The local camp tailor, Ghulam Nabi, was commissioned to equip the whole Battery with red trousers, which were worn off duty. During the middle weekend Major Bicknell led a band of Battery tourists to Beirut to celebrate his birthday. Meanwhile the remainder of the Battery enjoyed sailing, water skiing, lizard hunting and the various night spots of Cyprus. It was certainly a camp to be remembered.

The Battery returned to what was known as the quiet season. It was less quiet than in other years though. This was because two popular weddings took place, those of Jeremy and Celia Burroughs and Tim and Wendy Livingstone-Booth. On each occasion the Battery furnished a 'Rent a Guard' of Gunners in blues with gun rammers to form a triumphal arch for the happy couple. It is a fact that throughout 'C' Battery's entire existence both during the war and afterwards its members were continually being smitten by the charms of the fair sex. Skegness, Wantage, Cambridge, Ayr, Algiers, Rome, Florence, Monte Lupone and Klagenfeld all saw scenes of 'C' Battery Gunners in romantic action. Since the war the Battery Notes have been full of engagements and weddings. This is hardly surprising in view of the number of dances and parties which were held every year and of course the fact that many members were of an age when they were establishing themselves in their careers and love was in the air.

Although many people retired fairly soon after they became married, a number did not and it was important that their wives understood the nature of the HAC so that they would put up with its demands on their husbands' time. The support of the Battery's wives, and girlfriends as well, was an often forgotten but nevertheless important component of the Battery's *esprit de corps*.

It was also at this time that the BBC programme 'Man Alive' was shown, which featured the Territorial Army. A major part of the programme was about the HAC and viewers saw 'C' Battery firing a salute at the Tower of London. At the 1971 camp at Otterburn a composite HAC Battery commanded by Major Gilchrist trained for the Queen's Cup competition. This included a prominent number of 'C' Battery members. It was a bold experiment which resulted in a decisive win. After the camp Major Basil Bicknell handed over command of 'C' Battery to Major Bill Hebblethwaite. On his departure Major Bicknell donated to the HAC a painting he had commissioned of 'C' Battery firing the salute at the Tower of London.

Major Bill Hebblethwaite had been a regular RHA officer and had been posted as Adjutant to the HAC in 1966. He subsequently retired from the army and, finding himself working in London, remustered as a Gunner in 'C' Battery. As far as he was concerned it was the obvious choice. He was quickly promoted to become the last Battery Commander of 'C' Battery. For some time there had been rumours of further changes in the Territorial Army. These were finally announced in the summer of 1973 at the end of camp at Westdown. The Ministry of Defence decided to create a new role for the HAC which was defined as follows:

1. To provide two sub-units each of 108 all ranks, for an operational role in BAOR employing both artillery and infantry skills.
2. To provide two sub-units for home defence in the UK during war employing infantry skills.
3. To maintain a 6-gun battery in peace to assist in training the two sub-units at (1) above.
4. To provide Guards of Honour within the City of London and Saluting Batteries at the Tower of London.
5. To maintain an officer producing role.[6]

The new HAC unit consisted of four squadrons and the band, which were manned by a mixture of officers and men from both the Artillery Division and the Infantry Battalion. Thus all the old and beloved batteries and companies ceased to exist, although for tradition's sake each sub-unit was allocated to a squadron, which in 'C' Battery's case was 3 Squadron. This reorganization

Major Bill Hebblethwaite, Battery Commander 1971–1973.

caused a lot of heart searching at the time and some resentment, but it was in retrospect a wise decision in view of the dramatic nature of the change. It did mean, though, the end of 'C' Battery. The Battery had seen service for 34 years. It had survived numerous vicissitudes and reorganizations during that time and had always come up smiling.

The saying that old soldiers never die, they only fade away is alas not completely true. The Old Reaper invariably adds to his harvest every year. Brigadier James Grose MC had died in 1983, Brigadier Clive Usher DSO and Brigadier 'Tiger' Lyon-Smith DSO shared the same obituary page of *The Gunner* magazine in 1983, whilst Colonel Johnny Barstow DSO TD passed away in 1986. A number of post-war officers who served the Battery so wholeheartedly have also died. These are Major Tony Wenham TD, Colonel Brian Davis TD, Captain Richard Perring and Captain John Chandler. But there are others too whose absence from the ranks is felt at both the 12th Regiment's reunion dinners and the 'C' Battery dinners and parties which are still held from time to time.

Although it is nearly 20 years since the Battery's demise, its spirit still lives on, and on 13 October 1988, when the Long Room was filled for a dinner to commemorate the Battery's forthcoming fiftieth anniversary, the idea for this book was mooted. 'C' Battery will simply not lie down and be forgotten.

One post-war member actually found himself on active service. Ex-BQMS Guy

The wedding of John and Rosemary Burns on 4 September 1971. The file leaders of the Guard of Honour are Geoffrey Godbold (left) and Phillip Randall (right).

Edmunds moved to Rhodesia and in 1978 was manning an OP on the top of the Cecil Hotel in the middle of Umtali on the Mozambique border. The town came under mortar fire and Guy Edmunds was able to bring down accurate fire from a troop of 25-pounders, which silenced the opposition. After that he returned to the bar and thereafter had extreme difficulty in paying for a drink!

Two years later, on 20 November 1980, Basil Bicknell, pining no doubt for the 'C' Battery dances that he had helped to organize in the past, decided to organize an HAC ball in New York to raise money for the Armoury House Rebuilding Appeal. Thus in the presence of Their Royal Highnesses Prince and Princess

Michael of Kent, the ex-Colonel Commandant of the HAC, General Sir Rodney Moore, Lady Moore, and some 180 guests danced the night away and raised nearly £12,000 in doing so. It was good that the old ties between the wartime Allies were renewed and especially satisfying for the HAC to act as host to the Ancient and Honourable Artillery Company of Boston, who had given the HAC so much support during the dark days of the 1939–45 war. The Captain of the A&HAC, Captain Driscoll, with Mrs Driscoll, and two ex-Captains, Brigadier General James Lynch and Captain Ed Keelan, were among the guests.

How then is it possible to sum up the history of 'C' and to say whether it was indeed something special? The author asked one officer who had served in more than one battery of 12th Regiment what his opinion was. He replied that 'C' Battery was 'the liveliest battery'. This description would be equally appropriate for its post-war performance. It was not always the best at gunnery – 'A' and 'B' Batteries had their high standards too – but 'C' Battery was always the battery to beat. At every stage of its existence it possessed members of considerable talent and character and this small volume cannot possibly do justice to them all. After the war there was a lot of role playing in the Battery, members often went out of their way to appear to deprecate any kind of professionalism, but in fact, in doing so they probably worked harder than anyone else. Theirs was a sort of Corinthian ideal, typical of the British with their love of understatement. In fact the Battery was always very positive about its military competence and this was complemented by its enormous sense of fun, which made it such a satisfying and enjoyable unit to serve in. The Battery Commander, at all times during the Battery's existence, always knew he had the total support of his men.

Although 'C' Battery only exists in men's memories, the HAC still soldiers on, fulfilling an arduous and demanding role in support of the Regular Army. It is the spirit of the volunteer tradition in British society that is so important. Who knows but the time may come when the old gunner batteries and infantry companies of the HAC may be reconstituted, especially now 'the repressed demons of history are re-emerging in Eastern Europe in the general climate of disorientation and economic distress'?[7]

The average Briton has always had a love–hate relationship with his army – '... it's "Saviour of his country" when the guns begin to shoot', but cut the defence budget to the bone as soon as there is no foe in sight. That is why the Territorial Army plays such an important role in today's society. It acts as a vital bridge between the professional soldier and civilian life and also 'produces a core of men and women who respond to challenge, acknowledge values and imperatives beyond the purely selfish ones and are there to be called on'.[8] That surely was 'C' Battery's contribution, and with the 'shield of faith and the sword of the spirit' it did its duty. Others who follow its example will no doubt do theirs as well.

The Roll of Honour
'*C*' *Battery 12th* (HAC) *Regiment* RHA

North Africa

Gnr G.P. Bright	Constantine	18 Nov 1942
L/Bdr J.C. Keddie	Mateur	26 Nov 1942
Gnr P.E. Pickersgill	Nr Chouigui	30 Nov 1942
Gnr H.A. Voss	Nr Chouigui	30 Nov 1942
Gnr S. Winter	Nr Chouigui	30 Nov 1942
Gnr J.H. Newton	Beja	11 Dec 1942
Gnr E. Miles	Nr Mateur	13 Dec 1942
BSM R. Mackenzie	Bou Arada	18 Jan 1943
Gnr D. Cooper	Bou Arada	20 Jan 1943
Gnr S. Rimmer	Bou Arada	20 Jan 1943
L/Bdr A. Williams	Bou Arada	20 Jan 1943
Gnr G.H. Gould	Kournine	21 Apr 1943
Gnr T. Kenny	Kournine	21 Apr 1943
Bdr P.W.R. McGregor	Kournine	22 Apr 1943
Gnr F. Forth	Kournine	25 Apr 1943

Italy

L/Bdr H.H. Mash	Trocchio	14 May 1944
Gnr A. Patching	Trocchio	14 May 1944
Bdr W. Bennetts	Genezzano	4 Jun 1944
Lt E.C. Freeman	Genezzano	4 Jun 1944
Gnr A.H.M. Haynes	Genezzano	4 Jun 1944
Gnr T.M. O'Brien	Genezzano	4 Jun 1944
Gnr E. Gent	Frasinetto	5 Jul 1944
Gnr C. Turner	Frasinetto	5 Jul 1944

L/Bdr S. Gilchrist	Arezzo	3 Aug 1944
Gnr J.A. Mease	Montevarchi	3 Aug 1944
Gnr E.V. Phillips	Montevarchi	4 Aug 1944
Gnr R.A.J. Blackwell	Bocconi	11 Oct 1944
Gnr W. Young	River Senio	10 Apr 1945

Members of 'C' Battery who fell in action or died while serving with other units.

Capt. P.R. Alexander RA
2nd Lt H. Bonsall RA
Lt D.V.J. Boys RA
2nd Lt N. Carman, 3rd Royal Armoured Corps
2nd Lt L.J. Hotson, Royal Tank Regiment
Capt. G.C. Daniel RA
Capt. A.R. Forster RHA
Capt. D.S.Y. Garrett RA
Capt. C.S. Higgins, Black Watch
F/Lt F.D. Holdsworth RAF
L.J. Hotson RTR
Sgt J.R. Kettle, Int. Corps
Capt. R.H. Le Bas, 3rd King's Own Hussars
Capt. J.S. Loram MC RA
Lt G.J. MacPhee RA
Capt. R.H. Mills RA
Lt H.D. Mordle RA
F/Lt E.R. Muller-Rowland RAF
Capt. G.W.D. Ormerod RA
2nd Lt R.C. Pitt RA
Maj. H.G.StG. Pollock RHA
Lt C.F. Robinson RA
Capt. V.B. Thronsden RA
Lt J.O. Timms RHA
Lt J.G. Tyrell MC RAC
Lt W.C.O'D. Waddington RA
2nd Lt J.G. Wynne RA

Honours and Awards

The ranks given here are those held at the time the decoration was earned.

Military Cross
Major J.E. Grose
Major S.N. Rae
Captain H.N. Atherton
Captain J.M. Austin-Smith

Military Medal
Lance Sergeant G.A. Ferrari
Lance Bombardier E.C. Howes
Lance Bombardier R.H. Newell

Mentioned in Despatches
Major M.F. Gilbert
Captain K. Hunt (twice)
Captain P.K. Rooke
Captain E.J.V. Williams
Lieutenant T.N.W. Lacey
Lance Sergeant J.E. Farmer
Lance Sergeant G.A. Ferrari
Gunner B. Jackson
Gunner M. Manning

Honours awarded to officers who had served with 'C' Battery while serving with other units.

Commander of the Order of the British Empire
Brigadier T.C. Usher RA

Distinguished Service Order
Lieutenant Colonel T.C. Usher RA

Member of the Order of the British Empire
Major J.M. Beecham RA
Major A.E. Brown RASC
Captain D.J. Owen R Sigs

Military Cross
Major R.M. Clarke RA
Major A.G.P. Lincoln HAC RHA
Major P.E. Pettit HAC RHA
Captain D.H.E. Barber RA
Captain J.A.C. Baxter RHA
Captain H.A.P. Blamey RA
Captain R.E. Cartright RA
Captain J.A. Connell RA
Captain P.S.Y. Garrett (K) RA
Captain R.W. Harden 27th Lancers
Captain C.H. Harrison RA
Captain F.R. Holdsworth RA
Captain K. Hunt HAC RHA
Captain J.S. Loram (K) RA
Captain D.A. Low RA
Captain P.V. Lowe RA
Captain W.A. Taylor RA
Captain R.D. Tyler RA
Lieutenant A.E.W. Rumsey RA
Lieutenant D.T. Smith RA
Lieutenant J.G. Tyrell (K) RAC

Distinguished Flying Cross
Squadron Leader J.S. Adams RAF
Flight Lieutenant B.G. Carr RAF
Captain N.E. Chase RA
Captain J.P. Stunt RA

War Department Bronze Star (USA)
Lieutenant E.P.K. Willett RA

Chevalier of the Order of Leopold II (Belgium) with Palm
Major R.H. Forsyth RA

Croix de Guerre 1940–1945 (Belgium)
Major R.H. Forsyth RA

Military Medal for Valour (Greece)
Captain R.W. Harden 27th Lancers

'C' Battery 1939–1945

Below are listed names of those men who joined 'C' Battery in the early years of the war but did not remain with the Battery. The majority were commissioned and the list quotes officers' ranks, as far as they are known, as they were in 1945.

Adams, J.S. DFC Sq/Ldr RAF
Allen, P.A.L. Capt. King's Regt
Allesbrook, W.P. Lt RA
Anderson, A.I. Capt. RA
Archer, J. Capt. RA

Balkwill, B.D. Capt. RA
Balmer, B.R. Capt. RA
Barber, D.H.E. MC Maj. RA
Barne, I.M. RA
Barnett, A.H. Capt. RA
Barrell, V.W.G. Capt. RA
Baxter, J.A.C. MC Maj. RHA
Baylis, M.H. Capt. RD YEO A
Beale, W.H. Capt. Int. Corps
Bear, H.F. Capt. RA
Beaven, R.J. Maj. RA
Beecham, J.M. Maj. RA
Beecroft, B.R. Capt. RA
Berkeley, A.W.G. Capt. RA
Black, P.C. Capt. RA
Blake, L.G. Capt. RA
Blamey, H.A.P. MC Capt. RA
Blyde, P.C.G. RA
Boorer, P.I. Lt RA
Boustred, K.F. Capt. RA
Box, G.N. Lt Suffolk Regt
Braithwaite, M.W. RA
Brown, A.F. Maj. RASC
Brown, G.A. Lt RA
Brown, R.A. Lt RA

Brown, W.M.G. Lt RA
Bryett, P.A.
Bunn, R.H. RA
Carr, B.G. F/Lt RAF
Carter, D.M.
Carter, P.M.
Cartwright, R.E. MC Capt. RA
Carver, J.H. Capt. RA
Charles, M.G. Capt. 1st Gurkha
    Rifles
Chase, G.M. Lt RA
Chase, N.H. DFC Maj. RA
Chimes, G.E.L. Lt RA
Christian, G.C. Capt AD Corps
Church, B.E. Maj. R Sigs
Clark Rowland, R. RA
Clarke, R.M. MC RA
Cobley, R.G. F/Lt RAF
Cocksedge, R.E.C. Maj. RWK
Collett, A.W. Capt. RA
Connell, J.A. MC Capt. RA
Coote, E.S.
Creasey, R.H. Capt. RA
Cundy, N.W. Lt Indian Arty
Cunningham, H.J.I. RA

Daniel, R.E. Lt S Staffs
Danks, A.R. Capt. RA
Darton, J.H. Maj. RA
de Courcy-Thompson, S.B. RA
Donner, B.G.E. Lt RA

Drury, K.W. Lt RAOC
Duncan, K. Capt. RA

Edgar, E.J. Lt HAC RHA
Edwards, H.A. Maj. RAOC
Elgood, J.R. S Staffs
Elgood, L.R. Lt RA

Fairrie, J.N.E. Maj. R Sigs
Faker, H.V. Lt RA
Farrell, T.E.
Fastnedge, D.C. RA
Fishburn, K.C.F. RA
Flatt, K.E. Capt. RA
Fleming, B.L. Lt Col. RA
Flemming, J.A. Lt RA
Ford, G.R. Lt RA
Forsyth, R.H. Maj. RA
Fuller, J.C. RA

Garrett, A.Y. Lt Col. HAC
Gell, J.H. Capt. R Sigs
Godfrey, J.W.E. Lt HAC RHA
Goode, N.L.
Gorrod, B.L. Capt. RA
Gosling, L.S. Lt RA
Goss, J.T. Capt RASC
Gotz, P. Capt. HAC RHA
Grant, M. Capt. 27th Lancers
Griffiths, E.T.L. RA
Grumbar, R.J. Lt RA

Guerault, R.L.D. Lt 24th Lancers
Hague, J.N.
Hamilton, J.A.S. Maj. RA
Hampton, R.E. Lt RA
Harden, R.W. MC Capt. 27th
    Lancers
Harper, C.W. Maj. CMP
Harris, H.M. Capt. Int. Corps
Harrison, B. Lt Northants
Harrison, C.H. MC Capt. RA
Hellis, L.R.
Henderson, B.D. Capt. RE
Henman, R.S. Lothian Border
    Yeomanry
Hewett, J.E. Capt. RA
Hewitt, R.P.G. Capt. RA
Hick, G.A. Lt RA
Hickes, G.G.R. Capt. HAC RHA
Hill-Smith, S.R. Capt. RA
Holdsworth, F.R. MC Capt. RA
Hose, R.L.
Hughes, A.E. RA
Humberstone, D.T. Maj. RA
Hunter, J.A. Maj. RA

Ince, S.B. Capt. RA

Jackson, F.D. Lt RA
Johnston, A.H. Capt. RA

Keen, P.
Kelly, D.R. Maj. RA
Kelly, J.E.L. Capt. RA
Kemp, F.D. Lt RA
Kemp, R.S.W. RAC
Kennedy, F.D. RA
Kerridge, H.N. Lt RTR
Kiln, R.J. Maj. RA
King, S.H. Lt RA

Lawrence, A.E. RA
Lawson, R.M.A. RA

Leaman, G. Capt. RA
Lee, D.J. RA
Lewis, H.W. Capt. RA
Liddell, C.A. Capt. RA
Lloyd, P.H. Capt. RA
Long, J.R. Capt. RA
Loudon, D.G.S. Capt. RA
Low, D.A. MC Capt. RA
Lowe, P.V. MC Capt. RA

McGill, R.H.R. Maj. RA
McGrath, D.G.F. RA
McGrath, D.J. Maj. RA
McPherson, D.V. Maj. R Sigs
Manby, G.E. Lt King's Own
Mann, U.D.
Marks, F.M. RA
Marr, M.B. Capt. RA
Martin, F.M. RA
Masters, R.L. Capt. RA
Meek, H.N. Lt RA
Mitchell, C.W.E. Maj. RE
Modiano, B.I. Lt 13th/18th
    Hussars
Montague, P. RA
Mundy, J.S. Maj. RA
Murrell, A.R.A. RA

Newell, R.H. MM Capt. RA
Newman, P.V.
Nolloth, J.P. Lt RA

Owen, D.J. OBE Capt. R Sigs

Paine, G.
Parr, J.W. Capt. REME
Parsons, C.D. Lt RA
Partridge, G.M.
Picton-Turbervill, W. Lt RA
Pitt, R.
Plaisted, P.S.H. Capt. RA
Pocock, M.D. Lt E Surreys

Postlethwaite, T.W. Lt RA
Pritchard, H.B.A'B. RA
Provis, P.F. Lt RA
Pryde, W.K. Capt. RA

Reeves, J.E.
Reuss, B.L.L.
Reynolds, E. Capt. Int. Corps
Roberts, M.S. RA
Robinson, M
Rose, H.K.
Rowland, A. Lt RA
Rumsey, A.E.W. MC Maj. RA
Rustad, P.W. Maj. RA
Ryall, D.C.

Salter, J.H. Maj. RA
Samuelson, B.F.M. Capt. RA
Sanders, K.M. Maj. RA
Scarlett, G.W. Maj. RA
Seligmann, D.L. Lt RAC
Shaw, J.L. Maj. RA
Shepherd, C.F.H. Capt. RA
Sherston, E. RA
Shillaker, J.W. Lt RA
Slim, L.
Smith, D.T. MC Lt RA
Smith, R.V. RA
Stanley, P.V. Lt RA
Strang, J.H. RA
Streat, S.C.A. Lt RA
Stunt, J.P. DFC Capt. RA
Sunley, R.W.

Taylor, W.A. MC Capt. RA
Thomas, B.K. Lt Col. RA
Thomas, L.T. Capt. RA
Tritschler, A.E. Maj. S Staffs
Tucker, A.J.
Tyler, R.D. MC Capt. RA

Usmar, G.G. Capt. RASC

Wagner, J.M.
Walbancke, W.E.L.A. Lt RA
Weiner, D.P.C. Lt RA
Wellman, R.A. Capt. RA
Wicham, H.T. Capt. RASC
Wilkinson, R.D.P. Capt. RASC
Willett, E.P.K. RA
Williams, G.A. Capt. RA
Williams, H.B. Capt. R Sigs

Willis, A.E. S Wales Borderers
Wilmot, M.G.
Wilson, J.H.
Wilton, H.A. F/Officer RAF
Wisdom, A.S. R Sigs
Wishart, G.C. Lt Col. RA
Wolfe, G.B. RA
Wood, C.R. RA
Wood, H.R Capt. RA

Wood, W.P. Lt RA
Worley, F.C.McL.
Wycherley, K.F. Lt RA
Wyman, M.E. Capt. RA

Yeoman, M.E. Lt RA
Young, J.H. Capt. RA

'C' Battery 12th (HAC) Regiment RHA

The following is an alphabetical list of officers and men who served in 'C' Battery during the war. Names of those who were commissioned after serving in 'C' Battery are listed in Appendix C. Ranks quoted in this list relate to those held at the end of the war, with the exception of a number of officers who continued to serve afterwards.

Abbie, J.R. Gnr
Adams, H.C. Gnr
Alston, L.C. Gnr
Angus, D.D. Lt Col.
Ansell, B.R. Gnr
Ashpole, J. Sgt
Atherton, H.N. MC Capt.
Austin-Smith, J.M. CBE MC TD
    Col.

Bailey, B. Sgt
Barnes, G.N. L/Sgt
Bartholomew, T.W.M. BSM
Beaton, H. Gnr
Blackmore, C.W. Gnr
Blake, W.E. Gnr
Bogle, R. Gnr
Boorer, P.I. L/Sgt
Bowler, A.E. Gnr
Bradstreet, A.W. Sgt
Brinkman Gnr
Brough, J.H. Gnr
Brown, A.B. Bdr
Bryant, W.E. Sgt
Burns, W. Gnr
Burville, S.J. Gnr
Bushill, E.J. Gnr

Butcher, M.H. Sgt

Cain, A.B. Bdr
Campbell, I. Gnr
Campbell, J. Sgt
Campbell-Jones, O.C. Lt Col.
Carr, J.N. Sgt
Carter, J.E. Gnr
Chiverton, H.L. L/Bdr
Chubb, H.E. Capt.
Clegg, G.A. Gnr
Cole, A.D. L/Bdr
Collen-Jones, W.F. RQMS
Coster, S.G. Gnr
Curtis, A.J. Gnr

Davies, H.J. Gnr
Davis, R. Sgt
Day, F.C. Sgt
Denholm, T.B. Gnr
Derricott, J.E. BSM
Devlin, Gnr
Diamond, J. TD Maj.
Donaldson, G.L.S. L/Bdr
Doney, F.A. Gnr
Duffield, G.W. Bdr
Duncan, K. Capt.

Dunkley, A. L/Bdr
Dutton, C. Gnr

Earl, J.L. L/Bdr
Eccles, J. Gnr
Edwards, J.E. Capt.
Edwards, J.R.M. Gnr
Ellis, W.F. Gnr
Elmer, R. Gnr
Elphick, R.D. Gnr
Elwick, T.L. Sgt
Everrett, D.J. L/Bdr
Farmer, J.E. L/Sgt
Farmer, W. Gnr
Fergeson, L. Gnr
Ferrari, G.A. MM L/Sgt
Fletcher, W.H. Sgt
Ford, W. Gnr
Forestier-Walker, E.A. Capt.
Foulkes, R. Lt
Fowler, R. Gnr
Frost, J.D. Lt

Gamble, J.C. Sgt
George, M.L. BSM
Gilbert, M.F. CBE TD LLB Maj.
Gilchrist, S. L/Bdr

Gilkes, T. Gnr
Gollop, N.A.E. Gnr
Goodenus, C.F. Bdr
Goodman, A.B. Gnr
Green, D.H. Gnr
Greening, B.S. Gnr
Grice, T. Gnr
Grose, J.E. MC Brig.
Groves, B. Gnr
Grumbridge, R.P. L/Bdr

Haines, D. Gnr
Hall, J. Gnr
Hallett, W. Gnr
Hardiman, Gnr
Harper, G.S.C. Bdr
Harrison, A.C. Sgt
Harvey, M.E. Gnr
Hawkins, A. Gnr
Hawkins, W.L. 2nd Lt
Hellis, H.R. L/Sgt
Hendey, J.C. L/Sgt
Henley, L/Bdr
Hill, G.K. Bdr
Hobdell, R. Gnr
Hodges, C.G. 2nd Lt
Holland, S.H.D. Lt
Holt, A. Gnr
Horton, J.W. Sgt
Howes, E.C. MM L/Bdr
Hudspith, H.C.L. Bdr
Hudspith, S.G.A. Sgt
Huggett, W. Gnr
Hunt, K. OBE MC Brig.

Illingworth, W. Gnr

Jackson, B. Gnr
Johns, S.G. Gnr
Johnson, B. Gnr
Johnson, T.E. Gnr
Jones, W.A. Sgt

Keenan, Gnr
Kelly, J.W. Gnr
Kemp, F.H. Gnr
Kiernan, W. Gnr
Kilshall, J.H. Gnr
Knight, C.N. Sgt

Lacey, T.N.W. MBE DFC Lt Col.
Lakin, W.A. Gnr
Lamport, G.W. L/Bdr
Lawrie, W.O.
Lewis, A.K. Gnr
Lincoln, A.G.P. MC TD Col.
Little, W.J. L/Sgt
Lowe, G. Lt
Lowes, L.E.C. Gnr
Lunt, W.H. Gnr
Lyon, J.E. Gnr

McAndrews, J. L/Sgt
McCabe, J.G.J. L/Bdr
McCoskrie, J.S. Gnr
McKee, K.W. Gnr
Mackey, M.F. Gnr
McMenemy, J. Gnr
McPhail, N.C.
McPherson, P. Gnr
McStrafick, H. Gnr
Mairs, J. Sgt
Marchant, J. Sgt
Marr, M.B. Gnr
Marrows, F. Gnr
Martin, A.A. L/Bdr
Martineau, A.A. Gnr
May, J.C. BSM
Maycock, J. Gnr
Mease, J.A. Gnr
Metcalfe, H. Gnr
Middleton, E.S. Gnr
Miles, P.O. Bdr
Miller, I.G. Capt.

Montgomery, P. Gnr
Mooney, J.E. Gnr
Moores, G. L/Bdr
Moorhead, R. L/Bdr
Morris, D.E. Gnr
Murphy, A.W.G. Gnr
Murphy, M.J. Gnr
Murray, W.A. L/Bdr
Musson, E.H. Gnr
Myatt, R.D. Gnr

Nainge, B.W.T. BSM
Napier, A. Gnr
Newell, R.H. MM Capt.
Newell, S. Sgt
Nicholls, G.A. Gnr

Oates, A.E. Gnr
O'Brien, J.A. Bdr
Olive, S.A. Gnr
Oliver, H. Gnr
Ongley, P.B. Capt.
Osborne, H. Gnr

Page, A. Gnr
Parish, E.F.D. Gnr
Parley, I. Bdr
Partridge, G.N. Gnr
Pascoe, L.L. Gnr
Paterson, A. Gnr
Paterson, J. Gnr
Paterson, R.J. Bdr
Pearson, J.V.C. Lt
Pearston, J. BSM
Pettit, P.E. CBE MC TD Col.
Phillips, C.A. L/Sgt R Sigs
Piddington, E. Gnr
Pollen, F. Gnr
Pollock, H.G. St G. Capt.
Porter, C.R. Bdr
Priestley, H. Gnr
Pryde, W.K. Capt.

Purcell, W. L/Bdr
Purchase, G.W. L/Bdr

Radford, F. Gnr
Radford, N.H. DSO MC Maj.
Radley, G. Gnr
Rae, S.N. MC TD Lt Col.
Ramsey, C.L. Gnr
Remington, J. Lt
Richards, Gnr
Ricketts, F. Gnr
Roberts, H.L. Sgt
Rodwell, E.W. BQMS
Rogers, W.H. Gnr
Rooke, P.K. CBE Brig.
Rooke, W.H. Gnr
Rose, H.K. Gnr
Rowley, P. Maj.

Savage, J.E. Gnr
Scott, H.A. Gnr
Sheppard, G.H. Gnr
Shout, W.R. Gnr
Slater, W. Gnr
Smale, J. Gnr
Smith, A. Gnr
Smith, A.T.J. Gnr
Smith, E.A.C. Bdr
Smith, J. Gnr
Smyth, D.P.

Snaith, T. Bdr
Spence, G. Gnr
Spicer, L.A. Gnr
Spragg, R.P. Gnr
Stamp, W.C.
Starmer, F.G. Gnr
Steel, W.L. L/Bdr
Stephenson, F.C. Gnr
Sterling, G.E. Gnr
Stewart, W.S. L/Bdr
Stockham, B.J. Gnr
Stopper, M.M. Gnr
Suckling, H.D. Gnr
Summers, T.H. Sgt
Sumpner, L. Gnr
Swain, F. Gnr

Tanner, A. Bdr
Teadley, J. Gnr
Thomas, G.E. Gnr
Thomas, I.H. Gnr
Thorney, F.L. Sgt
Tighe, B.J. Gnr
Titterton, A. Gnr
Tolson, F. Gnr
Totton, J.M. Bdr
Tovell, W.J.V. Sgt
Tucker, A.J. Gnr
Turner, R.S. L/Bdr
Turner, W.P. L/Bdr

Usher, T.C. CBE DSO Brig.

Vallis, L.C. Bdr

Waite, C. Gnr
Ward, H.J. Bdr
Warne, R.M.M. 2nd/Lt
Wathen, M.G.W. 2nd/Lt
Watson, H.W. Gnr
Watts, K.P. L/Bdr
Webb, E.J. Gnr
Webster, R.N. Gnr
Wescombe, L.J. Sgt
West, L.A. Sgt
Weston, C. Pte
Wharton, H.E. Gnr
White, T.G. Gnr
Whitrod, J.D. Bdr
Whittle, L. Gnr
Williams, E.J.V. Capt.
Williamson, J. L/Sgt
Wilmot, R.W. Gnr
Wilmott, M.G. Bdr
Wilson, J.H. Gnr
Wilson, J.W. Gnr
Wood, W.H. Gnr
Writtle, Gnr

Yeo, W.D. L/Bdr

'C' Battery 1947–1973

The following is an alphabetical list of officers and men who served in 'C' Battery between 1947 and 1973. Dates refer to the time that individuals joined the Battery. Officers' ranks, as far as they are known, refer to the time when they retired from the HAC. Asterisks indicate those individuals who served in the war.

Agius, T.E.A. 1957
Allum, S.C. 1969
Anderson, M.B. 1962
Andrews, J.M.G. 1956
Archer, T.J. 1967
Ash, B.H. 1950
Ashcroft, P.B. 1961
Ashpitel, P.G. Lt 1956
Ashton-Jones, C.J. 1970
Attwood, J. 1950
Austin-Smith, J.M. CBE MC TD Col. 1947*

Baber, G.D. 1966
Babington, T. 1963
Bagshawe, R.T. 1958
Baker, R. 1948
Balfour, M.D. 1959
Ballantyne, H.R. 1956
Balmer, B.R. 1947*
Bambridge, D.C.N.
Barber, A.H. 1953
Barker, D.L.A. 1958
Barnard, R. 2nd Lt 1970
Barnes, W. 1963
Barns, N.F. 1961
Barrett, D. 1962
Barshall, P.F. TD Maj. 1947*
Bayley, 1951
Beale, M.Y. 1970

Bear, H.F. Lt 1947*
Bearn, J.R. 1949
Bell, P.B. 1961
Benson, A.H. 1955
Benson, R.J.S. 1963
Bentley, P. 1953
Berridge, A. 1949
Bickford, R.F. Lt 1948*
Bicknell, B.C. TD Maj. 1951
Biddle, D.F. 1959
Bird, J.L. 1953
Blake, M.G. 1970
Blomfield, A.H.L. TD
Blyde, P. 1949*
Boardman, I.M.W. 1970
Bodenham, J.F. 1973
Bomford, C.G. 1970
Borrett, D.M. 1963
Boyce, M. 1955
Bradshaw, J.R.W. 1963
Braithwaite, T.P.T. 1967
Brayton, 1951
Brind, R.P. 1965
Brook, N.K. 1956
Brooke-Webb, M.V. 1961
Brounger, H.I.S. 1955
Brown, A.C. 1968
Brown, M. 1948
Brunton, J. 1951
Bryceson, M.P.M. 1970

Burgess, R.S. TD 1953*
Burnell-Jones, I. 1951
Burnet, J.J. 1955
Burns, J.M. 1963
Burroughs, J.M. 1965
Buser, R. 1958
Buston, S.W. 1971
Butler, F.J. 1948
Butler, S.M. 1959
Butler, S.O. 1966
Butter, F.J. 1949

Caldwell-McGee, 1963
Carden, C.M. 1951
Carr, J.M.R. 1964
Carrington, W.D. 1957
Carter, P.H. 1970
Case, J.D. 1951
Cassidy, B.M.D. 1964
Cater, D.L. 1968
Cecil-Wright, R.P. 1960
Chalkley, P.A. 1960*
Chandler, J.L. Capt. 1951
Channer, A. 1967
Chapman, I. 1961
Chapman, T.C. 1956
Charlesworth, M.E. 1952
Clark, D.A.M. 1959
Clark, E.W. 1965
Clarke, N. 1964

Clayton, D.A. 1962
Cockell, M.H. Lt 1954
Collins, J.P.M. 1958
Colquhoun, J.I. 1959
Connell, M.S. 1960
Cook, D. 1948
Cooper, A.C. 1960
Cooper, L. 1959
Cooper, P.J. 1964
Cordingley, M.A.J.
Corke, P.W. 1965
Cosgrave, N.P. 2nd/Lt 1953
Cotterell, J. TD Capt. 1952
Courtenay-Evans, G.P. 1961
Coxe, C.A.M. Capt. 1961
Craddock-Henry, C.J. 1962
Craighead, C.I.R. 1960
Crispin, C. 1958
Croft, C.G.L.
Cross, E.C.T. 1951
Crothall, A.D. De G. 1955
Curran, B.T. Capt. 1957
Cutler, P.J.

D'Albiac, M.P.B. Lt 1951
Dale, A.C. 1956*
Dale, J. 1950
Dalgleas, A.P. 1960
Dams, S.I.O. 1964
Daniel, I. 1970
Daniel, M.W. 1961
David, I. 1967
Davies, A.P. Capt. 1947*
Davies, C.V. 1959
Davies, P.H.C. 1961
Davies, P.L. Capt. 1949*
Davies, R.I. 1953
Davis, B.L. TD Col. 1948
Davis, P.J.W. 1971
Dawson, I. 1953
De La Tour Willems, 1963
Delaunay, A.C. 1962

De Margary, A.M.
De Margary, G.D.M. Maj. 1972
Dickson, R.A. 1966
Dobbie, D.C. 1959
Dodd, G.D.M. 1963
Drysdale, I.D. 1966
Dunden, H.C. 1948

Ebden, W.M. 1964
Ebden, W.N.C. 1972
Edmiston, M.G. 1969
Edmunds, G.W. 1959
Edwards, J.E. 1948
Elphick, R.E. 1953
Emmerson, G.B. 1956
England, D.G. Capt. 1950
Ennis, A.M. 1963
Ennis, J.F. 1955
Evans, D.G. 1960
Evans, P.J.O. 1963
Evans, R.H. 1949

Fairbank, J.A. Capt. 1951
Farley, B.E. 1954
Farley, R. 1954
Ferguson, M. 1957
Few-Brown, P. 1953
Field-Phillips, P.H. 1961
Fieldus, J.N. 1960
Fischal, J. 1948
Flack, G.S. 1950
Fletcher, C.M.E. 1955
Fowkes, H.C.F. 1959
Francis, C.E.R. 1948
Franklyn, R.G.

Galgut, J. 1959
Galway, S.H. DeB. 1960
Gardner, 1948
Garland, D. 1959
Garth-Wilson, J. 1963
Gavin-Brown, I. 1962

Gibbs, M.G.C. 1960
Gibbs, N. 1953
Gibbs, P.D.E. 1962
Gibson, J.M. 1963
Gilbert, M.F. CBE TD LLB Capt. 1947*
Gilchrist, G.E. TD Col. 1956
Giles, 1963
Girling, D.M. 1955
Glencairn Campbell, D.C.B. 1965
Godbold, G.E. OBE TD Col. 1968
Goodchild, D.H. CBE 1953
Gordon, S.B. 1948
Gough, V.L. 1965
Granvill, J.R. 1951
Gray, I. 1959
Gray, R. 1952
Grear, P.A.P. 1965
Greathead, J.G. 1960
Greaves, G.B. 1961
Greenwood, J.S. 1960
Groom, J.R. 1971
Grout, N.A.B. 1951
Grubb, P.R. 1954
Gunz, T.W. 1959
Gurmey, P.L.G. 1949

Hale-Woods, E.J. 1956
Hall, R.D. 1951
Hallinan, E. 1958
Hamilton, N. 1966
Hamilton, N.L.J. 1962
Hannigan, J.C.G. 1966
Harbury, M.F. 1970
Hardie, M.S. 1953
Hardy, D.W. 1952
Hardy, N.A. 1970
Harman, R.J.R. 1960
Harris, R.H. Lt 1950
Hartigan, I.G.S. Capt. 1969
Hassell, J.K.K. 1958

Haysey, M.R. 1960
Hayward, B. 1969
Healy, D.E. Capt. 1962
Hebblethwaite, B.M. Maj. 1966
Henney, G. 1961
Hesketh, B.R.C. 1960
Hewetson, C.T. 1960
Higgs, W.V. 1956
Hill, D.W.K. 1960
Hill, J.C. TD 1967*
Hill-Smith, S.R. 1948*
Hills, T.J. 1963
Hilton, S.P. 1956
Hiscott, R.S. 1961
Hoare, R.Q. 1963
Hodgkinson, P.H. 1959
Hogg, M. 2nd Lt 1969
Host, C. 1970
Howe, P. St J. 1964
Hull, C. 1951
Hunt, W.G. Capt. 1971
Hyatt, G.O. 1966

Ingram, C.L.R. 1953

James, J.N.C. 1959
Jamison, D.L. 1968
Jarvis, M.W. 1971
Jenkins, T.B. 1957
Jenrick, L.H.D. 1951
Jinks, A.P. 1970
Johnson, K.P. 1969
Johnson, R.E.B. 1958
Johnstone, M. McA. 1950
Jones, J.S. Lt 1953

Kahn, D.J. 1956
Kalmar, M.V. Capt. 1950
Keene, J.V. 1949*
Kennard, N.R. 1964
Kilner, T.A.A. Lt 1955
King, P.J. 1963

Kingdom, R.G. 1965
Knight, J.R. 1956

Lachlan, S.D. 1973
Lambert, D. 1956
Lane, N.StJ.W.R. 1959
Langdon, J. 1949*
Latimer, D.C. 1961
Leahy, D.M. 1958
Levine, E. Lt 1955
Lewis, D.G. 1961
Lincoln, A.G.P. MC TD Col. 1947
Little, D.A.S. 1953
Livingstone-Booth, J.T. 1962
Loch, A.D. 1960
Logsdon, P.D.E. 1965
Long, P.H. 1960
Longcroft, J.G.S. 1960
Lovett-Turner, J. 1968
Lysaght, J.G. 1959

McCarthy, C. 1961
Macdonald, A.G. 1965
Macfarlane, I. 1952
MacNair, J.T.H. MC 1948*
Main, P. 1953
Mallam, W.D.C. 1959
Manson, A.A. 1949
Manson, M.P. 1972
Marshall, J.C. 1948
Martin, C. 1949
Martin, D. 1966
Mattey, D.G. 1965
Matveieff, N. 1958
Mayle, J.F. 1959
Mellotte, M.J.R. 1957
Mendham, G.E.A. 1950
Meredith, P. 1959
Millard, N.R.A. 1959
Miller, M.D. 1958
Milne, A.F.D. 1953

Mitford, J.P.B. 1973
Mizen, P. 1953
Moll, B.N.P. 1959
Monk, D.M.G. 1963
Morgan, C.E. 1956
Morgan, S.A.C. 1961
Morley, A.M. 1970
Morley, J. 1972
Morris, L. 1951
Morrison, H.R. 1966
Mortimer, A.G. 1961

Nalder, R.H. 1951
Neal, G.A. 1972
Neighbour, D.W. 1959
Newcombe, E.M. 1958
Newcombe, J.L. 1952
Newsome, A.J. 1972
Newstone, R.E. 1970
Nicholson, D. 1968
Nicholson, G.B. 1969
Nicholson, J. 1959
Nicol, J.S. 1963
Nikols, 1970
Norrington, N.C. TD 1965
Norris-Cowen, A. 1959
Norton, G. 1950
Norton, R.G. 1951
Nuthall, C.J.F. 1971

Oakes, R. 1950
O'Callaghan, L.V. 1956
Oliver, C.G. 1963
O'Neil-Donnellon, D.J. 1968
O'Rourke, C.J.A. 1959
Orpwood-Price, 1969
Overton, A.G. 1948
Owen, W.B. 1972

Page, J.W.M. Lt 1968
Paine, T.L. 1963
Parker, S. 1953

Parry-Wingfield, W.J. 1955
Parsons, R.J. 1963
Passmore, G.S. 1960*
Patmore, M.A.S. 1962
Pawson, E.K.L. 1960
Peacock, 1959
Peerless, B.R. 1955
Pengelley, R.B. TD 1969
Peploe, A.D.K. 1952*
Perks, C.G.E. 1952*
Perring, R. Maj. 1956
Peters, J.D. 1959
Philpott, B. 1970
Picton-Turbervill, W. 1948*
Platt, A. 1957
Playfair, R.D. 1955
Plunkett, D.A. 1960
Posner, G. 1951*
Potts, D.H. 1971
Powell, L.G. 1953
Powell-Brett, C.F. 1961
Powle, B.W. 1955
Prevost, B.T.G. Lt 1953
Prevost, W.R.V. 1959
Price, G.W.O. 1961
Prince, A.T. 1971
Prior, G.A. 1964
Prior, N.A. 1966
Prior, T.A. 1966
Pritchard, S.J. 1959
Pryce, E.L. 1959
Pugson, P.R. 1964
Putnam, G.A. 1957

Raffin, W.J.S. 1970
Randall, P.H. 1962*
Rankin, J.W. 1967
Ray, R.C. 1964
Reid, H.D.N. Lt 1961
Reney-Smith, J.F. 1970
Richardson, C. 1948*
Ridpath, J.H. 1956

Rising, W.T. 1968*
Robinson, M.E. 1967
Robson, K.F. 1960
Roche, J.P. 1965
Rochester, A.C. 1957
Roots, G.G. Lt 1962
Ropes, H. 1959
Ropes, J.J. 1960
Rose, H.K. 1948*
Rosenberg, W.P. 1947*
Rowbotham, A.V. 1960
Rowbotham, C.G. 1959
Rowe, W.N. 1948
Rushbrooke, R.V. 1959
Russell, B.S. 1950
Ryan, J.A.P. 1971
Ryves-Hopkins, K.M. 1958

St Giles, M.V. 1965
Sanderson, C.S. 2nd Lt 1970
Saunders, R.H.W. 1956
Sautter, M.J. 1961
Savory, C.J. 1962
Schofield, J. 1951
Scovell, T.A.J. 1954
Scrivener, M.J.H. 1951
Service, N.M.D. 1957
Sewell, J.A.F. MC 1947*
Sharman, C.T. 1960
Shepherd, B.D. 1948
Short, R.W. MM 1948*
Simpson, K.E. 1964
Simpson, R.M.J. 1951
Simson, J.N.L. 1970
Singer, A.R.E. 1971
Skewes, I.R.M. 1958
Skinner, J.G. 1968
Smeed, G. 1963
Smith, P.A.D. Maj. 1959
Smyth, A.B.J. 1960
Smyth, D.P. 1950*
South, W.M. 1970

Speers, C.J. 1966
Spicer, H.W. Lt 1970
Sprawson, 1969
Stacey, N.E.W. 1961
Stacey, N.P. 1973
Stevenson, A.W. 1965
Stewart, M.L. 2nd/Lt 1969
Stidolph, J.G.N. 1964
Stokes, C.N. 1954
Stone, P.M. 1962
Strachan, J.N. 1970
Strong, G.C. 1971
Suckling, P.J. 1952
Sugden, 1966
Swain, J. 1960
Sweny, P.H.H. 1962
Sykes, F.J.B. 1965

Tanner, A. 1949*
Tapley, D.A. 1959
Tapson, G.E. 1953
Taylor, D.J. 1959
Taylor, L. 1957
Taylor, M.R. 1960
Taylor, R.H. 1965
Taylor-Roberts, A.B. 1965
Temple, R.T. 1954
Tibbles, N.C. 1950
Tiley, R.B. TD Capt. 1953
Tilly, J.R.T. 1950
Tomkins, P.G.L. 1953
Trent, M.W. 1954
Truslove, T.W. 1951
Turner, R. 1948*
Tuson, A.B. Lt 1950
Tyler, T.J. 1954

Vale, L.F.B. Maj. 1960
Varden,
Vereker, N.H.P. 1960
Vernede, A.C. 1964
Vosper, J.P.E. 1963

Waddington-Shaw, I.M. 1959
Wadsworth, F.C. 1954
Waghorn, B.P. 1963
Walker, D.S. Maj. 1950
Walker, J.M.G. 1959
Wallace, P.D.B. 1953
Wallis, D. StJ. 1961
Walsh-Waring, P.H. 1949
Walter, R.J. 1961
Waples, B.L. 1953
Webb, E.J. 1949*
Webb, J.H. Lt 1957
Webber, D.J. 1949
Wellesley, R.A.V. 1959

Wenham, G.M. 1948*
Wenham, R.A. Maj. 1948*
Whaley, F.R. 1948
Whigham, J.M. 1963
White, B.W.B. 1967
Widdows, R.M. 1960
Wild, P.D. 1965
Willett, E.P.K. 1957*
Williams, C.C.U. Maj. 1953
Williams, E.J. 1960
Williams, M.G.W. 1948
Williamson, R.B. Lt 1970
Wilson, J.A.G. Capt. 1966
Wilson, J.H. 1950*

Wilson, L.T. 1963
Wilson, S.R.M. 1965
Wood, F.G. 1970
Wood, J.D. 1963
Wood, T.C. 1961
Wood, W. 1961
Woolnough, C.F. 1953
Wormald, J.R. 1957
Wormald,

Young, D.T. Capt. 1956
Young, R.D. Lt 1959

'C' Battery Commanders and Camps 1947–1973

Year	Battery Commander	Camp	Comments
1947	Major A.G.P. Lincoln MC TD	–	Recruiting commences
1948	Major A.G.P. Lincoln	Westdown	1st battery dinner
			1st royal salute at Tower
1949	Major A.G.P. Lincoln	Westdown	
1950	Major A.G.P. Lincoln	Bodney, Norfolk	National Service intake
1951	Major A.G.P. Lincoln	Tilshead Lodge	'Z' Reservists.
			1st 'C' Battery dinner
1952	Major J.M. Austin-Smith CBE MC TD	Sennybridge	1st battery dance
1953	Major J.M. Austin-Smith	Westdown	
1954	Major J.M. Austin-Smith	Westdown	
1955	Major J.M. Austin-Smith	Tilshead Lodge	
1956	Major P.F. Barshall TD	Rollestone	Field role
1957	Major R.A. Wenham TD	Sennybridge	
1958	Major R.A. Wenham	Sennybridge	
1959	Major R.A. Wenham	Epsom	Civil defence
1960	Major R.A. Wenham	Sennybridge	Threat of reorganization
1961	Major R.A. Wenham	Round Britain	
1962	Major B.L. Davis TD	Tilshead Lodge	Queen's Cup competition
1963	Major B.L. Davis	Westdown	Win Queen's Cup
1964	Major B.L. Davis	Westdown	
1965	Major B.L. Davis	Otterburn	
1966	Major B.L. Davis	Sennybridge	John Fairbank's death
1966	Major G. Gilchrist TD		Reorganization/AVR III
1967	Major G. Gilchrist	Folkestone	Greater London Regiment
1968	Major G. Gilchrist	Sennybridge	Unpaid camp
1969	Major G. Gilchrist	Rollestone	Battery reinstated with its guns
1970	Major B.C. Bicknell TD	Cyprus	
1971	Major B.C. Bicknell	Otterburn	Queen's Cup
1972	Major B.M. Hebblethwaite	Sennybridge	
1973	Major B.M. Hebblethwaite	Westdown	Reorganization and finale

Sources and references

CHAPTER ONE
1. Winston Churchill, *The Gathering Storm*, p.273.
2. HAC *Journal*, June 1939, p.293.
3. HAC *Journal*, July 1939, p.340.

CHAPTER TWO
1. Churchill, *op. cit.*, p.146.
2. HAC *Journal*, September 1939, p.410.
3. Lt Colonel S.N. Rae, *History of 12th* HAC *Regiment* RHA (unpublished), p.2.

CHAPTER THREE
1. Rae, *op. cit.*, p.3.
2. War Diary, 12th HAC Regiment RHA, PRO/WO 175-305.
3. Shelford Bidwell, *Gunners at War*, p.136.
4. *ibid.*, p.142.
5. Gordon Thomas, *Memoirs* (unpublished).
6. PRO/WO 175-305.

CHAPTER FOUR
1. On 2 July 1940, a British fleet opened fire on the French fleet in order to prevent it falling into German hands. Heavy casualties were inflicted and two battleships were accounted for. At Dakar, on 23 September 1940, an attack by the British fleet was beaten off by the French. The fierce fighting between the British and Vichy forces in Syria should also not be forgotten.
2. Dan van der Vat, *The Atlantic Campaign*, p.299.
3. The French fleet at Toulon consisted of 1 battleship, 9 cruisers, 29 destroyers, 16 submarines and other vessels. The majority were scuttled on 27 November 1942 (*The Official History of World War 2 [OHWW2]*, Vol.IV, pp.163–4).
4. The Americans lost 1404 soldiers and airmen killed, wounded or missing. The British lost only 89 men (*OHWW2*, Vol.IV, p.155).
5. Thomas, *op. cit.*
6. *ibid.*
7. The Barenthin Regiment was a Luftwaffe unit composed of staff and pupils of the Parachute School at Witstock and the Glider School at Posen (General Anderson's despatch, *London Gazette*, 6 November 1946).

CHAPTER FIVE
1. PRO/WO 175-307.
2. Rae, *op. cit.*
3. Anderson, *op. cit.*
4. Bidwell, *op. cit.*, pp.185–6.
5. Allan Lewis, *Memoirs* (unpublished).
6. John Horsfall, *Wild Geese are Flighting*, p.56.
7. *ibid.*, p.57.
8. Alan Moorehead, *African Trilogy*, p.520.
9. Colonel J.A.T. Barstow, letter quoted in HAC *Journal*, October 1943, p.13.

CHAPTER SIX
1. *OHWW2*, Vol.IV, p.460.
2. John Ellis, *The Sharp End*, p.181.
3. Rae, *op. cit.*, p.59.

CHAPTER SEVEN
1. J. Pickalkiez, *Cassino, Anatomy of a Battle* (quoted in John Ellis, *The Hollow Victory*, p.293).

2. *Royal Artillery Commemmoration Book, 1939–45*, p.315.
3. John Horsfall, *Fling our Banner to the Wind*, p.68.
4. Operations of 1st Guards Brigade, Cassino 4–18 May 1944: Intelligence Report.
5. Rae, *op. cit.*, pp.66–7.

CHAPTER EIGHT
1. Rae, *op. cit.*, pp.75–6.
2. Description of operations April/May 1945 by Colonel J.A.T. Barstow, quoted in Rae, *op. cit.*, p.4.

CHAPTER NINE
1. *OHWW2*, Vol.VI, pt 3, pp.334–5.
2. Quoted in the *Royal Artillery Commemoration Book, 1939–45*.
3. Thomas, *op. cit.*

CHAPTER TEN
1. HAC *Journal*, December 1951, p.76.

2. HAC *Journal*, August 1952, p.25.
3. HAC *Journal*, August 1955, p.275.
4. HAC *Journal*, August 1956, p.220.
5. HAC *Journal*, February 1958.
6. HAC *Journal*, December 1959.
7. Michael Miller, letter to the author.
8. HAC *Journal*, August 1961, p.230.
9. HAC *Journal*, *ibid*.

CHAPTER ELEVEN
1. HAC *Journal*, April 1966, p.156.
2. Tower Hamlets had been the home of 10th Rifle Brigade whom the Battery had supported in Blade Force.
3. HAC *Journal*, October 1968, p.171.
4. HAC *Journal*, October 1970, p.147.
5. *ibid*.
6. HAC *Journal*, August 1973, p.119.
7. *The Independent*, 25 November 1991.
8. HAC *Journal*, November 1971, p.198.

Bibliography

Armstrong, Geoffrey *The Sparks Fly Upward*, Gooday Publishers, 1991.

Beckett, Frank, *Algiers to Austria with the First and Eighth Armies*, Graphic Press (Grimsby) Ltd, 1986.

Bidwell, Shelford, *Gunners at War*, Arms and Armour Press, 1970.

Blaxland, Gregory, *The Plain Cook and the Great Showman*, William Kimber & Co. Ltd, 1977.

Bolton, Kenneth, *With the 11th (HAC) Regiment RHA*, HAC, 1945.

Carell, Paul, *The Foxes of the Desert*, Macdonald, 1960.

Churchill, Winston, *The Gathering Storm*, Cassell & Co. Ltd, 1948.

D'Arcy Dawson, John, *Tunisian Battle*, Macdonald, 1943.

Davis, Brian L., *The British Army in World War II*, Greenhill Books, 1990.

Ellis, John, *The Sharp End*, Windrow & Greene Ltd, 1980.

– *The Hollow Victory*, Andre Deutsch, 1984.

Ffrench-Blake, R.L.V., *History of the 17th/21st Lancers*, Macmillan, 1962.

Goold Walker, G., *Honourable Artillery Company 1537–1987*, Honourable Artillery Company, 1986.

Horsfall, John, *Wild Geese are Flighting*, Roundwood Press Ltd, 1976.

– *Fling our Banner to the Wind*, Roundwood Press Ltd, 1978.

Jackson, W.G.F., *The North African Campaign 1940–1943*, Batsford, 1973.

Johnson, E.F., *Regimental Fire!* Honourable Artillery Company, 1958

Kennard, George, *Loopy*, Leo Cooper, 1990.

Linklater, Eric, *The Campaign in Italy*, HMSO, 1977.

Lucas, James, *Panzer Army Africa*, Macdonald & Jane's, 1977.

Messenger, Charles, *Tunisian Campaign*, Ian Allen Group, 1983.

Moorehead, Alan, *African Trilogy*, Hamish Hamilton, 1965.

Pitt, Barrie, *The Military History of World War II*, Guild Publishing, 1986.

Playfair, Maloney & Jackson, *The Official History of World War II*, Vols. IV, V & VI, HMSO, 1966.

Roberts, G.P.B., *From the Desert to the Baltic*, William Kimber & Co. Ltd, 1987.

Rutherford, W., *Kasserine, Baptism of Fire*, Macdonald, 1971.

Strawson, John, *Battle of North Africa*, Charles Scribner's Sons, 1969.

van der Vat, Dan, *The Atlantic Campaign*, Hodder & Stoughton Ltd, 1988.

Honourable Artillery Company Journal 1939–1991

More Poems of the Second World War: The Oasis Collection, J.M. Dent & Sons Ltd, 1989.

The Oxford Book of War Poetry, Oxford University Press, 1986.

Royal Artillery Commemoration Book, 1939–45, G. Bell & Sons Ltd, 1950.

Unpublished accounts

Austin-Smith, Colonel J.M., Letters home 1939–1945

Barstow, Colonel J.A.T., *Mailed Fist Song Book*

Buttenshaw, Brigadier G.G., *Story of Blade Force, 13th Nov.–12th Dec. 1942* (Imperial War Museum)

Lewis, A.K., *Memoirs 1939–1943*

Lincoln, Colonel A.G.P., Letters home 1942–1943

Rae, Lt Colonel S.N., *History of 12th HAC Regiment RHA*

Thomas, G.E., *Memoirs 1939–1945*

Operations of 1st Guards Brigade, Cassino 4–18 May 1944: Intelligence Report

Abbreviations

AA	Anti-aircraft		OCTU	Officer Cadet Training Unit
AVR	Army Volunteer Reserve		OP	Observation post
AWOL	Absent without leave		OPA	Observation Post Assistant
BAOR	British Army of the Rhine		OTC	Officer Training Corps
BQMS	Battery Quartermaster Sergeant		RA	Royal Artillery
BRA	Brigadier Royal Artillery		RAC	Royal Armoured Corps
BSM	Battery Sergeant Major		RAOC	Royal Army Ordnance Corps
CMP	Corps of Military Police		RASC	Royal Army Service Corps
CPO	Command Post Officer		RA(TA)	Royal Artillery (Territorial Army)
CPO/A	Command Post Officer Assistant		RE	Royal Engineers
CRA	Commander Royal Artillery		REME	Royal Electrical and Mechanical Engineers
DSO	Distinguished Service Order			
ENSA	Entertainments National Service Association		RHA	Royal Horse Artillery
			RHQ	Regimental Headquarters
FOO	Forward Observation Officer		RQMS	Regimental Quartermaster Sergeant
GPMG	General purpose machine-gun		RSM	Regimental Sergeant Major
GPO	Gun Position Officer		RTR	Royal Tank Regiment
HAC	Honourable Artillery Company		RWK	Royal West Kents
HE	High explosive		SLR	Self-loading rifle
MC	Military Cross		SMG	Sub-machine-gun
MM	Military Medal		TA	Territorial Army
MT	Motor Transport		TD	Territorial Decoration
NATO	North Atlantic Treaty Organization		TSM	Troop Sergeant Major
NCO	Non-commissioned officer		WD	War Department
OBE	Order of the British Empire			

List of sponsors

This book could not have been published without the generous support of those whose names appear below and others whose contributions were received after going to press.

Angus, D.D.
Archibald, D.R.H.
Armstrong, G.R.
Atherton, H.N.
Attwood, J.
Austin-Smith, J.M.

Balmer, B.R.
Barker, D.L.A.
Barshall, P.F.
Basset, J.S.
Baylis, M.H.
Bear, H.
Beaven, R.J.
Beecroft, P.R.
Bickford, R.
Bicknell, B.C.
Biddle, D.F.
Bird, J.L.
Blake, M.G.
Bloomer, J.G.
Bloomfield, R.H.L.
Boosey, Mrs R.
Brook, N.K.
Burgess, R.S.
Burns, J.
Buston, S.W.

Campbell-Barnard, W.R.
Carden, C.M.
Case, J.D.
Cassidy, B.M.D.
Chapman, I.
Charlesworth, M.E.
Chase, N.H.
Cobley, R.G.
Collins, J.P.M.
Connell, M.S.

Cooper, A.C.
Cooper, L.
Cooper, P.J.
Corke, P.W.
Coxe, C.A.M.

Dale, A.C.
Daniel, M.W.
Darton, J.H.
Davidson-Smith, P.A.
Davies, J.G.M.
De Margary, A.M.
De Margary, G.D.M.

Earl, J.L.
Edmiston, J.S.M.
Edmunds, G.
Elphick, R.E.

Fairbank, Mrs J.
Farley, R.
Fowkes, H.C.F.
Frost, J.D.

Garland, D.
Garrett, J.P.
Gibbs, M.G.C.
Gibbs, P.D.E.
Gibson, Mrs A.
Gilbert, M.F.
Gilchrist, G.E.
Girling, D.M.
Godbold, G.E.
Goodchild, D.H.
Gray, R.G.
Grubb, P.R.
Grumbridge, R.P.

Hardy, D.W.

Harris, J.A.
Harris, R.
Harrison, H.W.P.
Hartigan, I.G.S.
Hassell, J.
Hayward, B.
Healey, D.
Hebblethwaite, B.M.
Henson, V.J.
Hill, J.C.
Hill-Smith, S.R.
Hills, T.J.
Hoare, R.Q.
Hunt, K.
Hunt, W.G.
Hyatt, G.O.

Irvine, I.A.N.

Keene, J.V.
Kilner, T.A.A.

Langdon, J.
Leahy, D.
Lee, T.D.
Lewis, D.G.
Lincoln, A.G.P.
Liscombe, R.M.
Logsdon, P.D.E.
Long, J.R.
Longcroft, J.G.S.

Macfarlane, I.
Macnair, J.T.H.
Madden, B.K.
Miller, M.D.

Nicholson, J.H.C.

O'Hagan, A.R.
Owen, W.B.

Page, J.
Parker, S.
Parsons, R.J.
Passmore, G.S.
Peerless, B.R.
Perks, C.E.
Perring, Mrs E.F.F.
Peters, J.D.
Pettit, P.
Pettit, P.E.
Picton-Turbervill, W.
Platt, A.
Playfair, R.D.
Posner, G.
Price, G.W.O.
Prince, A.T.
Prior, G.
Prior, N.A.
Purchase, G.W.

Rankin, J.W.
Richards, A.I.H.
Rising, W.T.
Robinson, D.N.
Roche, J.P.
Rochester, A.
Roots, G.G.
Rowbotham, A.V.
Rowbotham, C.G.
Russell, B.S.

Sanderson, C.
Schofield, J.S.
Scovell, T.A.J.
Seddon, J.
Shepherd, C.F.H.

Singer, A.R.E.
Skinner, J.G.
Spicer, H.W.
Stevenson, A.W.
Stokes, C.N.
Storer, J.H.
Strachan, J.N.
Swain, J.

Tapson, G.E.M.
Thomas, G.E.
Tiley, R.B.
Turner, R.S.
Tyler, T.

Vale, L.F.B.
Vereker, N.H.P.
Vosper, J.P.E.

Wadsworth, F.C.H.
Walker, D.S.
Webb, E.J.
Weiner, D.
White, J.W.
Williams, A.F.D.
Williamson, R.B.
Willis, A.E.
Wilson, J.H.
Wilson, S.R.M.
Wiltshire, J.
Wishart, G.C.
Wood, J.D.
Wynter-Bee, P.

Young, D.T.
Young, R.D.

Index

Emboldened references are to
illustrations.

1st Canadian Corps, 74, 77,
85, 90
6th S.A. Armd Div., 93

Abbie, J.R., 68
Adriatic, 81, 85, 87
Ain Draham, 57
Air OPS, 91, 93
Airburst, 76, 81
Alanbrooke, Gen., 21
Aldershot, 15
Alexander, Sir Harold, Gen.,
57, 60, 82, 90
Algeria, 29, 32
Algiers, 32, 33, 34, 46, 54,
69, 72
Altari, 80
Amazon Bridge, 75
Ammunition expenditure, 50,
55, 80, 87
Anacona, 87
Ancient & Honourable
Artillery Company, 122
Anderson, K.A.N., Lt Gen.,
46, 54, 66
Anderson's Circular Tour,
55, 56, 65
Angus, D.D., Lt Col., 3, 5, 9
Anzio, 72
Apennines, 81, 85, 87, 90
Aquino, 77
Arce, 79
Arezzo, 85, 89
Argenta, 93
Armoury House, 3, 4, 6, 100,
101, 102, 104, 105
Armstrong, G.R., Col., 103
Arno, 85
Arundel Castle, SS, 26, 29, 31
Ashcroft, P., 114
Ashpole, A., Sgt, 27, *66*
Askania, SS, 72, 74
Atherton, H.N., Capt., 27,
62, *68*, 76, 87
Atlas Mountains, 32
Attwood, J., 103, 107
Aubries Park, 16

Austin-Smith, M.J., Col., 9,
15, 26, 46, *68*, 69, 71, 75,
79, 80, 82, 89, 91, 92, 93,
100, 102, 103, 105, 106,
108
Austria, 2, 96, 97
Ayr, 25, 90, 109, 118

Bagnacallo, 91
Barnes, G.N., L/Sgt, 52, *66*
Barshall, P., Maj., 100, *103*,
108
Barstow, J.A.T., Col., 9, 18,
42, 46, 49, 50, 57, 61, 64,
69, 75, 93, 98, 100, 103,
120
Barstow, Mrs D., 106
Beirut, 118
Beja, 33, 34, 57
Bennett, J., 101
Bennetts, W., 81, 123
Bickerton, 109
Bicknell, B., Maj., 115, 116,
117, *118*, 119, 121
Biddle, D., 110
Bisley Hut, 102, 104, 117
Bizerta, 32, 33, 71
Blackwell, R.A.J., Gnr, 124
Blade Force, 30, 31, 33–44
Blue Angel, *107*
Bocconi, 87
Bodney, *103*
Bologna, 91
Bone, 33, 34, 54, 72
Borehamwood, 9
Bou Arada, 49, 51, 53, 56,
59
Bou Ficha, 62
Brazier, Sgt, 16
Bright, G.P., Gnr, 32, 123
British Army, 114, 116, 120
18th Army Group, 60
Army Volunteer Reserve,
114
Armies
Ist Army, 44, 56, 58, 59,
64
8th Army, 54, 57, 59, 60,
62, 71, 74, 89, 90, 91,
96

Corps
5th Corps, 60, 61, 85
9th Corps, 57, 60, 61
13th Corps (8th Army),
72, 76, 80, 85, 87
Divisions
1st Armd Div., 60
4th British Div., 75
6th Armd Div., 16, 21, 22,
24, 46, 48, 54, 55, 57,
58, 60–62, 66, 72, 79,
80, 81, 85, 87, 95, 96
7th Armd Div., 61, 71
78th Div., 30, 33, 34
Brigades
1st Armd Recce Bde, 16
26th Armd Bde, 55, 56,
57, 59, 62, 75, 79, *83*,
92, 93, 95
1st Guards Bde, 54, 56, 80
201st Guards Bde, 61, 62
11th Infantry Bde, 34, 37,
39, 41
36th Infantry Bde, 34
38th Irish Infantry Bde, 49
Royal Artillery, 8
2nd Regt RHA, 16
51st LAA Regt RA, 30, 41
72nd Anti-Tank Regt, 30,
39
104th Regt RHA, 87
132th Fd Regt RA, 40
136th Fd Regt RA, 103
138th Fd Regt RA, 24, 101
152nd (Ayrshire
Yeomanry) Fd Regt RA,
49, 51, 53, 71, 80, 100
160th Fd Regt RA, 9
252nd Manchester Arty
Regt RA (TA), 111
359th Medium Regt RA,
111
457th Light Battery RA, 40
851st (Westmoreland &
Cumberland) RA (TA),
111
Armoured Regiments
16th/5th Lancers, 25, 58,
59, 60, 72, 76, 78–82,
85, 86, 92, 93

17th/21st Lancers, 25, 30,
32, 34–36, 39, 40, 43,
48, 58, 62, 75, 85, 87
1st Derbyshire Yeomanry,
30, 34, 39, 62, 77, 78,
82, 95
Lothian & Border Horse,
25, 62, 75, 82
North Irish Horse, 55, 78
51st Royal Tank Regt, 57
Infantry Regiments
Argyll & Sutherland
Highlanders, 18
Coldstream Guards, 2nd
Bn, 47, 54, 57, 62, 80
Grenadier Guards, 3rd Bn,
53, 54, 57, 58, 79, 80
Gurkhas, 91
Hampshire Regt, 2nd Bn,
39, 40, 41
Lancashire Fusiliers, 2nd
Bn, 42–43
Leicestershire Regt,
2nd/5th Bn, 56
London Irish Rifles, 51, 53
Northamptonshire Regt,
5th Bn, 37, 39
Parachute Regt, 1st Bn, 42,
43
Parachute Regt, 3rd Bn,
33
Rifle Bde, 7th Bn, 87
Rifle Bde, 10th Bn, 30, 32,
34, 35, 36, 39, 48
Royal Inniskilling Fusiliers,
6th Bn, 48, 50, 76, 77
Royal Irish Fusiliers, 1st
Bn, 46, 49
Royal Scots Fusiliers, 18
Royal West Kents, 6th Bn,
33
Staffordshire Regt, 1st Bn,
115
East Surreys, 1st Bn, 40,
41
Welsh Guards, 3rd Bn, 57,
58, 62
Yorks & Lancs, 6th Bn, 60
Royal Engineers, 5th Fd
Sqn RE, 30

Royal Military Police, 26, 66
165th Light Ambulance, 30
Brockman, B., *107*
Brook, N., 106
Brothels, Algiers, 69
Bryant, W.E., Sgt, 27, *66*
Bubble and Squeak, 47
Builth Wells, 25
Bumper – Exercise, 21
Burns, A.H., Lt Col., 15
Burns, J., 121
Burroughs, J., 118

Cameronia, SS, 26, 29, 31
Campbell, H., Maj., 51
Campbell-Jones, O.C., Co'., 9, 11
Campo 49, 86, 100
Cassino, 74–77; *see also* Monte Cassino
Castel del Rio, 87, 90
Castel St Angelo, 74, 75
Casualties, 64, 68, 96
Causton, E.E.N., Maj., 60
Chamberlain, N., 2, 6
Chandler, J., *107*, 120
Charlesworth, M., 106
Chouigui, 37, 38, 40
Chubb, H.E., Capt., 27
Chudleigh, R.D., Lt, 93
Church of Scotland, 68
Churchill, Winston, 90, 97, 116
Churchill tank, 55, 57, 78, 90, 91
Civil Defence, 114
Clarke, D., 110
Clyde River, 26, 30
Cockell, M., *107*
Cold War, 110
Collect, Regimental, of HAC, 113
Collen-Jones, W.F., BQMS, 27, *65*, *66*
Compo rations, 47
Constantine, 32, 69
Cooper, D., 52, 123
Copeland-Griffiths, V., Brig., 54
Corke, P., 116, 117
Cossacks, 97
Court of Assistants of HAC, 2, 3, 4
Coxe, C.A.M., Capt., 109, 112, 115, 118
Cricket, 99, 105
Crocker, J.T., Lt Gen., 57
Crothall, D., 112
Crusader tank, 40, 47
Cyprus Camp, 117

Daniels, 104
Davies, A.P., Lt, 53, 100
Davis, B.L., Maj., 110, 112, 114, 115, 117, 120
Davis, R., Sgt, 27, *66*
Death Valley, 67
Depot Troop, 13
Derricott, J.E., Sgt, 27, 50, *53*, *66*
Dicomano, 85, 87
Djebel Abiod, 32
Djebel Bou Kourine, 60, 61
Djebel Maina, 40
Djebel Rihane, *49*, 57
Djedeida, 34, 37–40, 46
Driscoll, Capt. and Mrs A., 122
Dry Shod, 25
Dysentery, 67

Ecton, 15
Edmunds, G., 112, 121
Edwards, J., Lt, 48, *68*
Eilbote, 48, 53, 54
Eisenhower, D.D., Gen., 66
El Alamein, 48, 75
El Bathan, 38–40
Elkington, R.B., Maj., 34
Elphick, R., 106
Elwick, T.E., Sgt, 27
Enfidaville, 62
Ennis, J., 105
ENSA, 67
Eveleigh, Capt., 79

Faid, 33, 54, 55
Fairbank, J., Capt., 106, 112, 114
Farmer, L/Sgt, *66*, 67, 68, 81
Ferrari, G.A., L/Sgt, 27, *66*
Finale Dell Emilia, 93
Firenzuolo, 87
Fischal, J., Gnr, 102
Fischer, Genmaj., *38*, 39
Fletcher, W.H., Sgt, 27, *66*
Florence, 84, 85, 87, 89, 90
Focke Wulf 190, 36
Folkestone, 115
Fondouk, 33, 54, 55, 57, 58
Forestier-Walker, E.A., Capt., 27, 41
Forth, F., Gnr, 123
Foulkes, R., Lt, *68*
Francis, C.E.R., Sgt, 102
Freeman, E., Lt, 68, 81, 123
French troops, 30, 53, 72, 74
Frühlingswind, 54, 55

Gafsa, 33
Gari River, 74, 75, 77
Garland, D., 112
Genezzano, 80
George, M.L., BSM, 27

Gent, E., Gnr, 123
German Army, 36, 37, 38, 48, 62, 64, 96
German 10th Army, 90
Afrika Assault Korps, 54
Afrika Korps, 48, 57, 59
14th Panzer Corps, 93
5th Panzer Army, 48
1st Parachute Corps, 93
1st Parachute Div., 76, 77, 79
10th Panzer Div., 38, 53, 55, 56
21st Panzer Div., 55
Goering, Hermann, Div., 60
90th Light Div., 62
334th Mountain Div., 53
7th Panzer Regt, 53
Barenthin Regt, 42
Jäger Regt Hermann Goering, 49
Germany, 2, 29
Gilbert, M.F., Maj., *86*, 100, *103*, 105
Gilchrist, G., Col., 115, *116*, 117, 118
Gilchrist, S., L/Bdr, 124
Girling, D., *105*
Godbold, G., Col., 117, *121*
Gothic Line, 81, 85, 86
Goubellat, 48, 59, 60
Gould, G., Gnr, 60, 123
Goums – Les Goumières, 53
Graham, P.L., Lt Col., 18, 19, 24, 25
Grandstand Hill, 49, 50
Grapeshot, 91
Graves, War, 42, 106, 107
Grose, J.E., Brig., 25, 27, 32, 34, *39*, 40, 41, 44, 120
Grousers, 93
Gunnery/gun drill, 12, 22, 23, 109
12-pounder, 29
18-pounder, 6, 11, 12, 14, 16
18/25-pounder, 12
25-pounder, 16, 29, 69, 70, 71, 121
4.5" Howitzer, 12, 14, 16
105mm, 81
Priest self-propelled gun, 70, *78*, 82, 87
Sexton 25-pounder, self-propelled gun, 90, *91*, 106
Gurk, 97
Gustav Line, 72, 74, 76

Hammam Lif, 62
Hammamet, 62, 66
Harrison, A.C., Sgt, *66*

Harvey, M., Sgt, 37, 56
Haynes, A.H.M., Gnr, 81, 123
Healey, D., Lt, 116
Hearsey, Capt. (Padre), 42
Hebblethwaite, B.M., Maj., 115, 119, *120*
Hellis, H.R., L/Sgt, *66*
Hendey, J.C., L/Sgt, *66*
Heseltine, G.R.N., Lt Col., 9, 10
Hill-Smith, R., BSM, *101*, 103
Hitler, Adolf, 2, 72, 95
Hitler Line, 74, 76, 77, 78, 80
Holland, S., Lt, 68
Honourable Artillery Company (HAC)
1st Bn, 105, 110, 114, 117, 119
1st Regt HAC RHA, 100, 101, 103, 106–11, 114, 119
3 Squadron HAC, 119
'A' Battery, 2, 6, 98, 100, 102, 109, 114, 115, 117, 122
'B' Battery, 2, 100, 101, 102, 114, 116, 122
12th (HAC) Regt RHA, 2, 6, 9, 10, 14, 16, 21, 25, 46, 48, 57, 58, 60, 61, 62, 64, 66, 69, 72, 74, 75, 76, 80, 81, 82, 85, 87, 90, 91, 92, 93, 96, 98, 106, 120, 122
W Troop, 14, 26, 32, 33, 34–36, 37, 42, 57, 62, 76, 87
X Troop, 26, 33, 36, 42, 43, 46, 47, 50, 57, 64, 68, 71, 76, 81, 93
'D' Battery, 2, 9, 14, 18, 48, 49, 53, 55, 56, 60, 75, 81, 87, 97
'F' Battery, 14, 18, 48, 49, 53, 55, 56, 60, 71, 75, 81, 82, 97
11th (HAC) Regt RHA, 2, 59, 66, 98, 103, 109
13th (HAC) Regt RHA, 18
86th (HAC) H.A.A. Regt RA, 2
Hospital, 67, 69
Hudel Battle Group, 38, 40
Hudspith, S.G.A., L/Sgt, 27, *66*
Hughes, D., Maj., 68
Hull, R.A., Col., 30, 43
Hunt, K., Brig., 40, 42, 48, 51, 56, 62, 64, 65, *68*
Hurricane, 37

Indian troops, 72
8th Indian Div., 75, 80, 90
Italian Army/troops, 36, 62
Italy, 54, 87

Jardin D'Essai, 32
Jaundice, 67
Jefna, 34, 35
Jock Cup, 109, 111, 113, 117
Juin, Gen., 77
Junkers 87 (Stuka), 37, 39, 41, 52
Junkers 88, 34, 36, 37, 38

Kahn, D., 106
Kairouan, 54, 59
Kalaat Djerda, 56
Kangaroos, 91
Kasserine, 33, 34, 54–56
Keddie, J.C., L/Bdr, 34, 123
Keelan, E., Capt., 122
Keene, J., BSM, 103
Keightley, C.F., Gen., 54, *69*
Keitel, German Chief of Staff, 2
Kenny, T., 123
Kensington, 105
Kesselring, Field Marshal, 38, 72
King George VI, 21, 26, 67, 102
Klagenfurt, 97
Knight, C.N., Sgt, *66*
Koch, 38, 40
Ksar Tyr, 61

La Bohème, 89
Lacey, T.N.W., Lt Col., 27
Lakenheath, 21
Lamport, G., Gnr, 98
Larkhill, 16, 102, 109
Latham, H.B., Brig., 26
Lazenby, G.V., Maj., 9, 15
Le Kef, 33, 55, 56
Leave, 89, 98
Leighton Thompson, C.E., Rev., 115
Lewis, A., 31, 54
Libya, 48
Lilac Blossom, 60
Lincoln, A.G.P., Col., 27, 33, *35*, 34–37, 40, 41, 42, 46, 47, 48, 55, 58, 60, *68*, 71, 100, 102, *103, 104*, 106, *107*
Lincolnshire, 14
Liri Valley, 77
Livingstone-Booth, T., 116, 118
Longcroft, J., 112
Longstop, 33, 47, 60, 64
Lovibond, J., 109

Lowe, G., Lt, 68
Lüder Battle Group, 38, 39, 40
Lynch, J., Brig. Gen., 122
Lyon-Smith, T., Brig., 19, 24, 43, 60, 62, 66, *69*, 71, 120

McAndrew, J., L/Sgt, 27, *66*
McGregor, P., Bdr, 60, 123
MacKenzie, R., BSM, 27, 50, *52*, 123
MacLeod, D.S., RSM, 13, 14
Macerta, 87
Mail, 46
Mailed Fist Song Book, 45
Makarios, Archbishop, 117
Maknassy, 54, 55
Maktar, 54
Malaria, 67, 68
'Man Alive', 119
Mansell, G.W., Lt Col., 26, 42, 46
Marchant, G., Sgt, 27, *66*, 68
Mareth, 54
Masaryk, 98
Mash, H.W., Gnr, 76, 123
Mateur, 32–34
Mease, J.A., Gnr, 82, 124
Mediterranean, 30, 32, 33
Medjerda River, 33, 34, 46, 61
Medjez-el-Bab, 33, 34, 41, 46, 47, 60, 61, 64, 106
Mepacrim, 67
Mercier, J., *105*
Merstham, 107
Messerschmitt 109, 36
Middleton, C., Maj., 60
Mike Target, 23
Miles, E., 43, 123
Miller, I.G., Capt., 27, 54
Mines, 53, 58
Mirabello, 93
Monte Cassino, 74, 76, *77*
Monte Grande, 79, 80
Monte Lignano, 85
Monte Lupone, 89
Monte Piccolo, 79
Monte Trocchio, 74, 75, 77
Monte Vesuvius, 74
Montgomery, B.L., Gen., 21, 48, 54
Moore, Sir Roger, Gen., and Lady, 121
Moorehead, A., 58, 59
Morgensluft, 54–55
Mortars, 81cm, 117
Mortleman, E.A., Maj., 9
Munich, 2
Murray, H.B., Maj. Gen., 85, 95, 96
Murray, W.A., Sgt, *66*
Mussolini, 71, 95

Nabeul, 66
Nabi Ghulam, 118
Naples, 71, 74, 89
National Service, 103, 104, 110
Naumann, A., Lt, 36
Nazi Party, 96
Nehring, Gen., 38
New Zealand Div., 9
Newell, R.H., Capt., 27, 51
Newell, S., Sgt, 52, *66*
Newton, J.H., 43, 123
Nightingales, 75
Nix, C., Maj., 58

Oakes, R., Gnr, 103
O'Brien, J.A., Sgt, *66*
O'Brien, T.M., Gnr, 81, 123
Ochsenkopf, 56
OCTU 121 RA, 9, 15
OCTUs, 15
Officer Training Wing, 110
Ongley, P., Capt., *68*
Opera, 89
Otterburn, 109, 119
Oued-Zarga, 41
Oxford University Training Corps, 116

Page, R.S., RSM, *105*
Panzer Mark IV, 40, 51
Patching, A., Gnr, 76, 123
Pearston, W., Sgt, 16, 27, *66*
Peel-Yates, D., Sir, Lt Gen., 115
Pennell's Camp, 107
Penthièvre, 66
Peporana, 93
Perring, R., Capt., 111, 120
Perring, R., Sir, 111
Perugia, 82
Pesaro, 90, 85
Pettit, P., Col., 11, 16, 19
Phillips, C.A., Sgt, 27, *66*
Phillips, E.V., Gnr, 124
Phillipeville, 66
Pickersgill, P.E., 37, 123
Picton-Turbervill, W., 3, 105
Piedimonte D'Alife, 74
Piumarole, 74, 77
Platt, A., 112
Playfair, R., 107
Plumbers, 56, *58*, 59
Plumbers' Mates, 56, *59*
Po River, 91, 93, 95, 96
Point-279, 49, 50, 51
Point-286, 49, 50, 51, 52
Polish Army, 74, 76, 85
Pollen, F., Gnr, 52
Pollock, H.G.St G., Maj., 27, 36, 124
Pontassieve, 83
Pontedina, 90
Posner, G., 106

Prince and Princess Michael of Kent, 123
Public schools, 110, 111

Queen Mary, 16
Queen's Cup Competition, 111, 119
Queens Road Station (Battersea), 10

Rae, S.N., Lt Col., 27, 32, 37, 41, 47, 48, *50, 68*, 75, 80, 81, 86, 98
Ramsey, C.L., 52
Randall, P., BSM, *121*
Rigoletto, 89
Rimini, 81, 85
Rimmer, S., 52, 123
Robaa, 33, 53
Roberts, G.P.B., Maj. Gen., 57
Robertville, 66, 67, 71, 72
Rohia, 56
Rollestone, *116*, 117
Rome, 72, 80, 81, 89
Rommel, 48, 53, 54, 56
Rooke, P., Capt., *68*, 71
Rose, H.K., Gnr, *101*, 102
Rosenberg, W.P., 102
Rotherhithe, 11
Round Britain Camp, 109
Rowbotham, A., 112
Rowbotham, C., 112
Rowland, G., 15
Rowland-Clark, R.C., 13
Royal Navy, 25, 32
Royal salutes, 101, 115, 119
Rugby football, 24, 68, 102, 105
Running cross country, 23, 115

Sabkrat el Kourzia (Sugar Lake), 60, 61
Sakiet Sidid Youssef, 57
Salerno, 71
San Benedetto, 84, 86
San Domenica, 89
Santerno River, 84, 92
Sbeitla, 54, 55
Sbiba, 33, 54, 55
Sbikha, 59
Scott, A., Gnr, 68
Scrivener, M., *107*
Sedjenane, 33
Senegalese troops, 31
Senio River, 90, 91, 92
Sennybridge, 21, 108, 109, 115
Sewell, J., 103
Shelford, 23, 25
Sherman tanks, 57, 71, 87, 90
Sicily, 34, 54, 71
Sidi Bou Zid, 54

Sidi Nsir, 32, 34
Sillaro River, 84, 92
Skegness, 14
Skews, I., 110
Skins, *see* Royal Inniskilling
 Fusiliers
Sloughia, 46
Smyth, D., 24
Snell, D., Lt, 116
Soccer, 24, 68, 97, 105
Souk-Ahras, 32, 33
Souk-el-Arba, 33
Spitfire, 33, 91
Stack, Col., 56
Stalin, 97
Steamroller Farm, 57
Stephenson, F., 52
Stewart, M., 116
Stokes, C., 106
Strassburg, 97
Stymie – Exercise, 25
Sudbury, 16
Sudetenland, 2
Summers, T.W., Sgt, 27, *66*
Surrey Docks, 11
Sutling, 108, 109, 112
Swain, J., 110
Syndicate, 112

T Roads, 34, 42
Tangier, 31

Tapson, G., 110
Tebourba, 33, 34, 37, 38, 39,
 40, 41, 46
Teboursouk, 33, 42, 43, 46
Templar, G.W.R., Maj. Gen.,
 85
Territorial Army, 2, 8, 100,
 103, 110, 111, 114, 119
Testour, 46
Thala, 33, 56, 90
Theatre, *67*
Thetford, 109
Thomas, G., Gnr, 24, 37, 68,
 95
Tiber, 82
Tilshead Lodge, 104, 112,
 138
Tito, 97
Titterton, A., 68
Tower Hamlets, 114
Tower of London, 101, 105,
 115, 119
Training, 4, 6, 9, 12–14, 18,
 19, 21–25, 72, 74, 101,
 102, 111, 114, 115, 117
Trasimene, Lake, 82
Trieste, 97
Tunis, 29, 30, 33, 37, 44, 46,
 47, 60, 61, *64*, 66, 95
Tunisia, 32, 33, 54, 89, 90
Turner, C., Gnr, 123

Two Tree Hill, 48, 53, 59,
 60, 61
Tyler, T., *107*

U-Boats, 30, 31
Uncle Target, 23, 50, 62, 80
US Army/troops, 54, 72, 74
 US 5th Army, 78, 82, 85,
 91, 93
 1st US Armored Regt, 34,
 39, 40
 34th (Red Bull) Div., 57,
 58
 American Combat
 Command Group 'B',
 41
 US 92nd Div., 82
US Air Force, 61, 62, 90
Usher, C., Brig., 19, *20*, 23,
 24, 79, 90, 102, 120

Valentine tank, 40
Velden, 96
Victory in Italy Day, 95
Victory parade in Tunis, 64,
 66
Villa Frasinetto, 85
Villa Gentili, 86
Von Arnim, J., Colgen., 48,
 54, 56
Voss, 37, 123

Vulcan, 60, 61
Vulnerable points (VPs), 9,
 114

Walker, D.S., Maj., *105*, *107*
Wantage, 16
Webb, E.J., *101*, 102, 103,
 105, 112
Webber, D.J., 102
Weitensfeld, 97
Wenham, R.A., Maj., 102,
 103, 109, 110, 120, 138
Westcombe, L.J., Sgt, 27, *66*
Westdown, 102, 103, 111,
 119
White, T., 68
Widdows, R., 112
Williams, A., L/Bdr, 52, 123
Williams, E.J.V., Capt., 87
Wilson, J.F., Maj., 24
Wilson, J.H., 105
Winter, S., L/Bdr, 52
Wood, D., 116
Woodage, V.S., L/Bdr, 52
Woodward, F., Capt., 68

Young, D., Capt., 110, 112,
 115
Young, R., Lt *68*
Young, W, Gnr, 91, 124
Yugoslavia, 96, 97

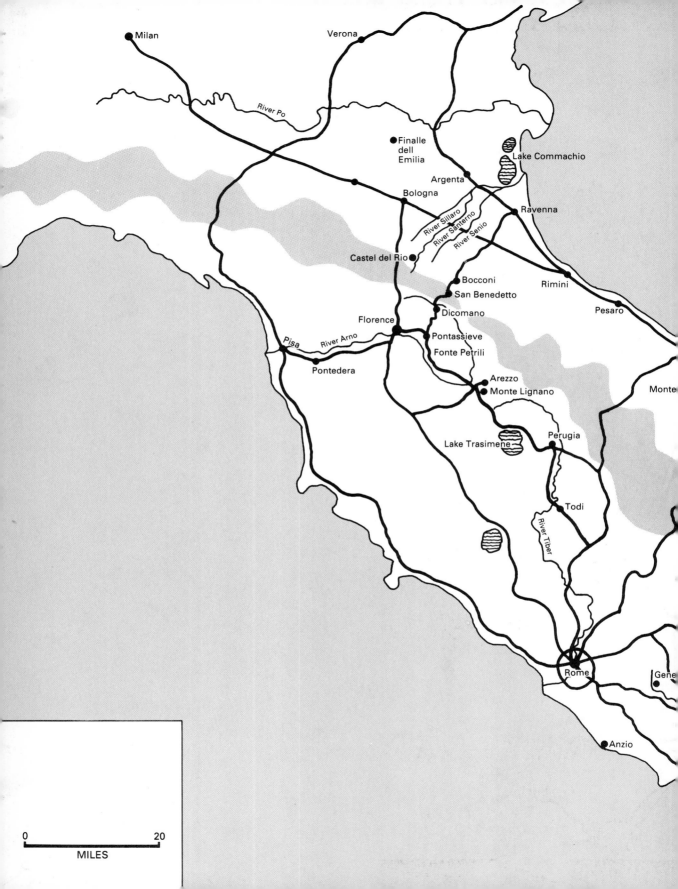

Milan

Verona

River Po

Finalle
dell
Emilia

Lake Commachio

Argenta

Bologna

Ravenna

River Sillaro

River Santerno

River Senio

Castel del Rio

Bocconi

Rimini

San Benedetto

Dicomano

Pesaro

Florence

Pontassieve

Pisa   River Arno

Fonte Petrili

Pontedera

Arezzo

Monte Lignano

Monte

Lake Trasimene

Perugia

River Tiber

Todi

Rome

Gene

Anzio

0   20

MILES